THE YEAR-ROUND SCHOOL

THE

YEAR-ROUND SCHOOL

The 45–15 Breakthrough

Kenneth L. Hermansen
and
James R. Gove

LINNET BOOKS

1971

Published 1971 by Linnet Books,
an imprint of The Shoe String Press, Inc.
995 Sherman Avenue
Hamden, Connecticut 06514
© 1971 by School Calendar Revision Institute
Romeoville, Illinois

ISBN-0208-01169-2
Library of Congress catalog card number 70-146655

Contents

Preface

No single subject in education today has received more talk, with less action, than the Year-Round School.

This highly controversial but intriguing proposition moved from the talk stage to the action stage on August 15, 1968. On that date, the Board of Education of Valley View School District 96, of Romeoville and Bolingbrook, Will County, Illinois, passed a resolution directing its school administrators to implement a year-round school calendar program two years hence. School enrollment was then 4,942—up from 89 in fifteen years. But nearly 7,000 kindergarten, primary, intermediate, and junior high school students were expected to enter the school system before the end of the 1970-71 school year, for which the Board directed implementation of the year-round calendar.

On June 28, 1970, the first of 6,603 Valley View students entered classes in what has turned out to be an entirely innovative concept of the Year-Round school. It differs radically from the dozens of year-round plans that have been suggested, but never implemented, over the past 30 years.

Let us make clear from the start that the Valley View 45-15 Year-Round School plan is not an educational experiment. It is a way of life—one that the authors expect will be continued in District 96 for years to come. When District 96's Board of Education directed its administration to proceed with a year-round school calendar, it was faced with a serious crisis in school administration. The calendar revision was dictated by seemingly insurmountable conditions. The School District had completely exhausted its bonding power. In addition to an almost unbelievable geometric progression in enrollments, it was faced with a new crisis created by the Illinois Legislature. In 1968, the 75th General Assembly made kindergarten mandatory in all public schools in the State. To District 96 this meant imposition of an additional classroom load of more than 800 kindergarten age children on what was already an overburdened school plant.

In studying the feasibility of a year-round calendar plan, the administration estimated that calendar revision could be effected in three years. The Board of Education, however, faced the reality of the housing crisis brought on by the pending arrival in September, 1970, of a continuing onrush of kindergarten students. Brushing aside the caution of the administration, the Board members voted on August 15, 1968, that the year-round plan must be implemented by the 1970-71 school year, when the kindergarteners would arrive.

The administration had already embarked on an intensive study of the voluminous published literature available on year-round calendar plans. Review of the available bibliography revealed one salient fact. Most commentators were concerned, not with making new calendar programs work, but with arming administrators and teachers with objections and arguments to combat the pressures for year-round schools. These pressures originated primarily with businessmen and trade and taxpayers' organizations. The proponents wanted to adopt what seemed to be, on the surface, an entirely reasonable and workable business proposition.

With the two-year deadline a reality, the Valley View administrators faced the task of researching, developing, and implementing a viable and acceptable plan that would meet the needs of the student body and would also win the acceptance and cooperation of the faculty and the Community. The administration's research made abundantly clear that *none* of the dozens of plans that had been proposed previously would be workable in the Valley View District, or would be acceptable today in any other school system.

It was necessary for the administration to cast away all previous concepts of year-round school programs, and to develop a workable calendar of its own. In less than 60 days of "cut and fit" experimentation with theoretical calendars, the administration evolved the "45-15 Year-Round School Plan." This was placed in effect on June 29, 1970.

This book is essentially a case history written for the guidance of other school administrators, for board members, and for citizens

interested in bringing economy, accountability, and educational efficiency to their schools. It will hopefully provide administrators and
board members with an accurate chart for navigating the admittedly
troubled waters of pioneering in a new phase of school administration.

The book is divided into three parts:

I. The first five chapters are devoted to the history and state of
the art. They simply collect, condense, and evaluate the voluminous
literature that Valley View found to be most helpful in formulating
calendar revision plans. The purpose of these chapters is to save the
time of those who may be considering the year-round school because
a decision regarding calendar revision appears to be advisable. This is
the "talk" part of the book. It presents all of the arguments, pro and
con, and explanations of the many varieties of year-round calendar
proposals.

II. Chapters six through twelve are largely narrative. They record
the evolution of Valley View's 45-15 day plan; the legislative, policy,
and administrative steps that were necessary to bring the 45-15 plan
to fruition; and the day-to-day problems of planning, faculty relations, community communications, and management that brought
the plan to the working stage.

III. Chapters thirteen through sixteen are essentially an appraisal
after the fact. The Valley View administrators look objectively at
their solutions, failures, and successes. This section, the authors
hope, will prevent many headaches, plus hours, days, and weeks of
"spinning the propeller" for those who are considering venturing on
what are really uncharted seas.

The actual writing of the book has presented special problems to
the authors. As working administrators charged with the day-to-day
decisions, actions, failures, and successes, they had difficulty in preparing an objective presentation and evaluation. They realized that
the editorial "we" was inappropriate. It was then decided that the
book should be couched entirely in the third person. This meant that
the authors would be actors on the stage, but that they could speak
through most of the book from the omniscient viewpoint of the
playwright or the novelist.

In October, 1970, the first year of 45-15, the authors and their
associates in the Valley View schools began an intensive series of
tape-recorded interviews that searched every aspect of the District's
experience. These continued well into 1971. Members of the Valley

View staff and faculty talked at length, and frankly, with an educational writer selected to resolve the apparent problems of viewpoint, organization, and objectivity that the creation of the book presented. This writer is Hal Burnett, of the *Park Forest (Illinois) Star,* a suburban community chain newspaper, who has reported on school administrative matters for more than 35 years.

The authors and the writer wish to express their indebtedness to the following:

The many pioneering educational thinkers who have talked about, and attempted to work out, year-round school calendars, especially during the last fifteen years of intensive school building expansion.

An inspired Board of Education. Members serving during the development and implementation of 45-15 were the late Bernard Ward, James Bingle, William Butchart, Erenesto Edsall, George Hassert, Kenneth Kibbler, Harold Lindstrom, Robert Noethen, John Strobbe and Bruce Webster.

All of the members of the Valley View District 96 staff—especially John Lukancik, assistant superintendent; J. Patrick Page, director of research; Ronald N. Strahanoski, director of curriculum; and to the principals and teachers who have accepted the plan so enthusiastically, made it work, and contributed their thoughts to the book.

The children of all school ages, and their parents, who embarked on the 45-15 program with enthusiasm and trust.

Robert Norfleet, of Hinsdale, Illinois, the educational consultant who applied his skills as a systems analyst to working out for elementary schools the previously unsolved problems of computer scheduling of classrooms, teachers, students, and buses efficiently in a complex learning situation.

Dr. Richard W. Hostrop, of Homewood, Illinois, a community college president and educational and editorial consultant, who contributed guidance and judgment to the manuscript.

The authors welcome questions, suggestions, comments, and criticism from the administrators, teachers, and citizens who read these pages.

Kenneth L. Hermansen
James R. Gove

Romeoville, Illinois
April 1971

THE YEAR-ROUND SCHOOL

1

Breakthrough

"Gee, Mom. Next year I get four vacations!"

With this note of delight, ten year old Christy Ward, of Boling-brook, Illinois, carried home to his mother official notice of a major breakthrough for year-round education.

Christy gave his mother a neatly typed, three-inch by five-inch index card. It read:

```
Christy Ward
176 Pinecrest

You will attend North View School next year.
Your first school term begins September 1.
Registration and regular classes will be held on that
day.

Have a good vacation.

                                            N-4
```

The cryptic "N-4" in the corner identified Christy's assignment to the fourth grade at North View. Only this code, and telltale perforations on the edges, revealed that Christy's individual notification card had been "printed out" by a computer. Or that 6,601 other students and enrollees of Valley View School District 96, of Will County, Illinois, had received similar cards the same day.

Two weeks later, on June 30, 1970, the five primary schools and one junior high school in Valley View District 96 opened their doors to 1,696 students, from kindergarten through eighth grade. These were the pioneer members of Group "A," the children who were destined to follow the first of four rotating "tracks" throughout the remainder of the school year. District 96 had embarked on its unique, compulsory "Valley View 45-15 Year-Round School Plan."

Group "B," containing 1,457 students, started classes Tuesday, July 21, just three weeks and one day later. They started on a Tuesday, instead of on a Monday, because the school calendar had been set back one day by the celebration of Independence Day on Friday, July 4.

Group "C," containing 1,751 of the students enrolled in the District, entered school on Tuesday, August 11, three weeks later. All six schools were filled virtually to capacity.

On Monday, August 31, the members of Group "A" completed their first "quarter" of 45 working school days, and returned to their homes for a three-week, fifteen-day vacation. The next day, September 1, their classroom seats were occupied by the 1,608 members of Group "D," the only Valley View students who enjoyed a full, traditional three month vacation in the summer of 1970.

Valley View had begun the first of its four teaching cycles that would continue through the 1970-71 school year. The fourth group, "D," was destined to complete its four quarters of instruction, sandwiched between three vacations of fifteen school days each, on August 16, 1971

COMPULSORY YEAR-ROUND SCHOOL

For the first time since 1938 all of the students of a United States public school system were attending school under a legally compulsory, year-round plan.

In the opinion of members of the community, the Board of Education, the school administrators, and the teachers, the Valley View 45-15 day plan is already a success.

"We have undertaken the program because of necessity, and we shall be forced to live with it for years to come," the superintendent reported to the board.

Valley View's 45-15 day plan is radically different from the score or more year-round school plans that have been proposed and debated by laymen and school administrators during the past fifteen years.

It is also radically different from the "nine-month, three-month" plan that was carried out by the schools of Aliquippa and Ambridge, Pennsylvania, between 1928 and 1938.

Like Aliquippa and Ambridge, the Valley View plan had its origins in a shortage of classrooms. It was undertaken primarily as a school "housing" device. Valley View had exhausted its power to issue bonds to finance sufficient school buildings to care for its anticipated enrollment. In addition, the Illinois General Assembly had voted that all public schools in the state must institute compulsory kindergarten in the fall of 1970.

Moving decisively in late July, 1968, the Board of Education urged the superintendent of schools to move "with all haste," to prepare for a year-round school program to be instituted in 1970.

The Board flatly rejected the two alternative solutions as "educationally unsound" and "totally unacceptable to the Community." The alternatives were:

1. To increase the class size from its present average of 24 to 36 or more.

2. To institute "double sessions" of half-day classes.

The latter solution was considered to be particularly unpopular with the Valley View District voters, because it was being followed currently in the Lockport West High School, which serves most of the communities in elementary District 96.

The administration immediately rejected the "nine-month, three-month" plan, which had failed in Aliquippa and Ambridge during the thirties.

"It was obvious to us that parents will never accept any plan that calls for four three-month vacations in the four sessions of the year," the superintendent told the Board. "It is simply impossible to co-ordinate the vacations of working parents with the convenience of the school. Besides, what mother would put up with mud and snow in the kitchen for three months in midwinter. The parents would crucify us."

MIDWINTER VACATION ELIMINATED

The fact that the three-month vacations in midwinter, fall, and spring were unpopular with the steel industry workers in the two Pennsylvania communities was responsible for the ultimate demise of the nine-month, three-month plan there.

Seeking to overcome the paramount objection that made both the Pennsylvania plans (and all other nine-month, three-month plans) unacceptable to parents, the Valley View administration turned, in September, 1968, to the possibility of alternating nine *weeks* of classes with three *weeks* of vacation.

Such a plan, if workable, appeared to offer these advantages:

1. It would be more palatable to parents, since it would be possible to adjust most normal two-week or three-week vacations to one of the three-week vacation periods in a family's school schedule. (Failing this, the school could reasonably shift the children in a family to another school "track.")

2. Theoretically, at least, it would reduce the school system's capital investment in school buildings by $5 million or $6 million, since they could accommodate one-third more students in existing buildings during the school year.

3. It would also be educationally sound. Gone would be the long, three-month lag in formal learning that takes place during the normal three-month summer vacation, with the demonstrable setback in the student's grasp of the school curriculum. (Most teachers devote the first month of school of the fall term to reviewing the subject matter presented in the previous spring.)

4. It would offer teachers the opportunity to increase their annual earnings by one-third, thus obviating the necessity for their seeking nonprofessional employment during vacations.

5. It would theoretically fulfill the Illinois School Code's requirement for a minimum of 176 school days, after allowing four days for teacher "institutes" and "snow holidays."

Unfortunately, the nine-week, three-week plan actually did not fulfill the Illinois statutory requirement for guaranteeing 176 days of classes. The trouble was that the school calendar was interrupted too often (ten times a year) by national, school, and religious holidays.

DAYS, NOT MONTHS

Pat Page, District 96's research director, was instructed to go back to his calendars. In mid-October of 1968, he came up with the answer—a 35-foot-long visual presentation of a school calendar that was based on *days*, rather than weeks or months. He had arrived at the proposed 45-15 day calendar by working backwards from September, 1971—the month in which the eighth grade graduates would have to enter freshman classes in Lockport West High School. He had preserved the traditional Christmas and Easter holidays, although shortening them slightly, and had allowed for an additional break of twelve calendar days, or ten school days, from June 24 through July 5, 1971.

The administration and the School Board recognized that this solution was workable, and that it could be "sold" to the Community. However, the school system was destined to embark on an intensive 21-month period of planning, legislation, and communications with the Community and the school staff before the 45-15 day plan could be implemented on June 30, 1970.

A discussion of this period of preparation, and the problems that were faced, and solved, makes up most of this book.

The Valley View administration had no time to conduct a comprehensive "feasibility" study, such as those undertaken by some school systems, usually with negative results. However, it did explore in depth the extensive literature on the subject of year-round schools, calendar revision, or extended school years. The Valley View collection of literature on the subject fills a full file drawer. Most of the contents are arguments pro and con—businessmen and laymen in favor of year-round schools, and school administrators opposed. The next chapters will give the reader an "overview" of this literature—a summary of the various plans proposed, and a condensation of the many arguments pro and con.

2

Origins

There is nothing sácred about the traditional nine-month school year and three-month vacation common in the United States.

It is essentially a vestige of an agrarian society in an age when the country has become 93 percent urbanized. In the first half of the 19th century, the major cities all had school years approaching eleven months. In 1840, for example, New York held classes for 49 weeks; Chicago for 48 weeks; Buffalo, 50 weeks; Cleveland, 43 weeks; Detroit, 259 days; and Philadelphia, 252 days.

By contrast, many rural schools were open for classes only six months out of the year.

This discrepancy may be explained by analyzing the respective needs of the communities involved. In the middle of the 19th century, the United States was inundated by a series of migrations from the European countries and Ireland. A very substantial portion of the adult population in the cities was composed of first generation immigrants, who spoke no English. German, Italian, Swedish, and other tongues native to Europe were spoken in a major share of the homes. Children, on the other hand, needed to adjust to a society that was gradually becoming Americanized.

The most important subject in the curriculum at every grade in the urban elementary and high schools was English; children needed to know English, to become bilingual, in order to adjust to their new environs, and to maintain their ties with the "old folks." Frequently both parents worked for a living, in mills, factories, and small professional shops. The students needed to attend school for the full year in order to acquire skill in the English language before they joined their parents as child laborers. There were few day care centers, and no baby-sitters. Parents needed to "park" their children in school, to be sure that their activities could be accounted for. Hence the predominance of school calendars of eleven months, or more, in the major industrial cities.

RURAL HERITAGE

Rural problems were different. The earth was tilled and cultivated by human labor, assisted by horses and oxen. Every member of the household had to work from sunup to sundown to plant the crops, to cultivate them, and to reap the harvest. Cows required milking at dawn and dusk. Wells were dug by hand; water drawn by hand. There were no tractors or harvest combines; the internal combustion engine had not been invented. There was little the child needed to know that he could not learn from his father and mother. From early childhood he joined in their tasks and labored in the fields throughout the long spring, summer, and fall days. Schooling, in a nearby church, or a one-room rural establishment, was confined to the winter months.

Gradually, during the last half of the 19th century, adequate schooling became the concern of state legislatures, and public education became the subject of increasing regulation in state constitutions and state school codes.

Although legislatures were predominantly rural, both urban and rural leaders were concerned to guarantee equal opportunity to the country and city children. The industrialized society and life on the farm were becoming more mechanized. There was need for greater emphasis in the schools on mathematics, science, and the history and geography that were so important in welding together a national society. Both elementary and secondary education became more formalized as the handful of church-related private colleges along the eastern seaboard were supplemented by a growing number of agricultural and mining colleges and land grant universities throughout the nation. A college education became many a child's goal. Obviously there must be uniformity of curriculum and preparation to prepare each student as equally as possible for entry into college.

As education became more rigid and state controlled, the legislatures worked compromises between rural and urban needs in their state codes. Minimum curriculum standards were imposed, and more important, the number of hours and days of public schooling was set by law in the proliferating school codes. Gradually, during the first quarter of the twentieth century, the school day became standardized with a legal minimum of 180 school days a year, established in most state codes. Many of the large cities, however, exceeded the state statutory minimums, offering from 190 to 195 days of school.

240 DAYS IN EUROPE

It is interesting to note, in passing, that the United States, with its passion for universal education, still offers substantially fewer days in school than do the nations of Europe, Asia, and Latin America. Austria, Czechoslovakia, and Denmark each offer 240 days in class to their students. The Soviet Union schedules 231 days of classes; West Germany 233. Even India has 200 days of school in elementary grades, and 205 days in its equivalent of our high school. Of modern nations, only Italy, with 154 days of elementary and secondary education, falls below the 180-day calendar that has become virtually standard through the United States since World War I.

There has been some demand for calendar reform ever since the present school year became stabilized. Bluffton, Indiana, placed a rotating "four quarter" program in operation in 1904, primarily to provide housing for all of its children. But no records remain today of the plan's success.

Another significant experiment in changing the school calendar was instituted by Dr. William Wirt, the highly controversial, but pioneering, superintendent of the Gary, Indiana, school system, in 1905.[1]* Gary's problem was similar to that of many eastern cities; the "new town" had a population that was then largely foreign-born. There was reason to emphasize schooling and to provide school "housing" for working parents. Wirt instituted what he called the "platoon" system, "parking" children in auditoriums, cafeterias, and gym and pool bleachers between their various classes. Even first and second grade children moved in droves from classroom to classroom, the antithesis of the self-contained classroom common in primary grades during the past four decades. Elementary and secondary schools were conducted in the same building and equipped with unusually large community facilities, which served adult education and recreation at night.

*Superior figures refer to the bibliography found on page 152.

One of Dr. Wirt's innovations was what he called a "year-round school." In reality, it was a pure summer school, conducted on a voluntary basis. Its objectives were to accelerate the movement of pupils through the grades, particularly nine through twelve, to enable them to enter the work force sooner; also to offer some degree of "enrichment." Dr. Wirt was years before his time; his educational reforms were not universally popular with the community, and he departed from the "Steel City" in 1907. With him went the summer school, and many other innovations.

Between 1910 and 1925, various forms of year-round schools were organized in a dozen cities. Among them were Albuquerque, New Mexico; Amarillo, Texas; Ardmore and Tulsa, Oklahoma; Bayonne, New Jersey; Elveleth, Minnesota; Mason City, Iowa; Minot, North Dakota; Nashville, Tennessee; and Omaha, Nebraska. Some of these were instituted because of a shortage of school facilities, others because of a desire to increase the school curriculum, or to accelerate progress through school, and to facilitate an early entrance into the work force.

NEWARK'S ENRICHMENT

Probably the most significant "year round" school experiment of the teens and the twenties was that in Newark, New Jersey. Newark began an experiment in summer school operation in two schools in 1912, and ultimately expanded it to include the complete system in 1921.[2]

In Newark, the school calendar was organized on the four-quarter plan. Attendance was compulsory for the fall, winter, and spring quarters, and optional in the summer. As in Gary, Indiana, the dominant problem was concern for the second generation children of foreign-born parents. The primary goal was to increase these children's use of the English language. A second was to prepare them for earlier entrance into the work force. It was felt that the extra learning in the summer months would give the children of foreign-born parents a better chance of progress during the remainder of the school year. For the first time, an effort was made to employ consultants to assess the success of the "year round" program. Consultants found that the all-year schools held many students in school until graduation from high school who otherwise might have become "dropouts" because of their difficulties with English. It was felt that many students worked through the fourth quarter with early grad-uation as a goal. Some of these students were graduated from high school at thirteen and fourteen, instead of sixteen and seventeen, and were in reality no better prepared than if they had taken their sum-mers off. The school board found that these accelerated students of foreign heritage were still ill-equipped as to language and other aca-demic subjects. Also, the School Board and administration reasoned, these early graduates were not sufficiently mature to enter the work force. By 1931, the Newark program ran into community dis-affection and was abandoned.

Nashville, Tennessee, adopted a continuous four-quarter plan, similar to Newark's, in 1922.[3] At the peak, the summer enrollment reached approximately two thirds of that in the winter quarters. Summer enrollment was especially heavy in the black sections of the city. The summer term was to be utilized for additional work (i.e. enrichment) or to make up unsatisfactory work during the previous three quarters. An evaluation of the Nashville program by the George Peabody College for Teachers indicated that students attending the summer quarter did no better than those not attending. Possibly this was a result of high attendance by disadvantaged blacks. However, a tangible gain was the fact that many students advanced further in their education than they would without the summer quarter plan. This program was abandoned in 1932.

DIFFERING GOALS

The significant common denominator of the Bluffton, Gary, Newark, and Nashville programs was the primary objective of increas-ing the learning available to the student body—in particular to offset the educational disadvantages of children of minority descent. More schooling for the disadvantaged was a laudable goal, but it was not universally popular with taxpayers. It is important to note that all of these programs were abandoned at the onset of, or during, the "Great Depression" of 1933-39. The public was not ready to pay for "enrichment" with tax money. The authors of this book believe that few communities today are willing to dig down in their pocketbooks to publicly finance an expansion of the educational program. Hence, most "fourth quarter" or "summer school" programs that survive today are financed primarily by tuition charges, and secondarily by some formula of state aid.

Entirely different goals governed the actions of the school boards in Aliquippa and Ambridge, Pennsylvania, both of which instituted "multiple track" four-quarter programs in 1929 and continued them through the thirties–depression years. Both cities were the sites of steel plants–Jones & Laughlin in Aliquippa, and American Bridge (U.S. Steel) in Ambridge. Aliquippa was the first of the two communities to institute a "four-quarter" school; it continued the program the longest (until 1938), and its conduct of a year-round school was researched most fully.

The Aliquippa and Ambridge experiments are interesting and important because they were conducted for the same reason that is motivating the serious efforts in calendar revision today. This is the widespread need to "stretch the building dollar" by fuller utilization of existing school facilities.

H. R. Vanderslice, then superintendent of Aliquippa schools, in 1930 attributed the community's action to three dominant reasons:[4]

1. There was a pressing need for school buildings in a town that had seen its school enrollment rise from 2,292 in 1919-20 to 6,611 in 1928-29.

2. The School Board desired to secure greater utilization of the school plant, which had cost more than $1,530,000 in the big dollars of the twenties.

3. There was also a feeling that there were many students in the district who should have the opportunity to continue their schooling throughout the year to place them on an equal footing with their peers.

In addition, the Aliquippa superintendent pointed to the advantage of using the fourth quarter as a "makeup or review period" for students who had fallen behind their classmates. The Aliquippa superintendent listed still further corollary benefits:

1. Children who were overage when they entered school would have the opportunity of attending school all four quarters, completing in one year what they might normally accomplish in one year and three months.

2. Ambitious boys and girls who wanted to graduate from school early, in order to enter the labor pool, could also attend school for four quarters. (However, the Aliquippa administration was reluctant to advance younger children to earn their diplomas before their 17th birthdays, holding that this would be permitted only after thorough consultation with the parents.)

3. It was possible to arrange for one older child in a family to stay at home during each of the four quarters, thus making it possible for mothers to hold paying jobs.

4. It was easier for older boys to find vacation work in industry, when their vacations fell in the fall, winter, and spring. (The school system worked out a "co-operative" program for older boys, who spent their off-season working in the steel mills.)

5. The school band was kept organized throughout the summer months, thus giving the community entertainment at a season when it would be most appreciated.

Vanderslice, in writing for school journals of the day, brushed aside the disadvantages of scheduling vacations during the off seasons of the year "When all of the facts concerning family vacations are brought together," he wrote, "it will probably be found that only a small percentage of the population cannot be accommodated by careful assignments of pupils to school periods, after consultation with parents. . . ."

The Aliquippa superintendent wrote that a simple rearrangement of the calendar plan had enabled the high school to accommodate 2,200 pupils in 1933 compared with the theoretical educational capacity of 1,650 pupils. The school calendar allowed for two weeks' vacation for everyone at the beginning of July.

The quarters were scheduled to begin on July 15, October 10, January 15, and April 10 of each year. This made sure that the vacation quarters fell during the four seasons of the year. Extra time was allotted between quarters. All parents had the option of vacationing during the first two weeks of July, even though their children's vacation quarters fell at different times of the year.

SAVINGS $201,877 ANNUALLY

Turning to economics of the plan, Vanderslice estimated that savings of the Aliquippa plan over five years averaged $201,877 annually. A third of this saving was attributed to debt service, and one third to savings in teachers salaries. (These savings, of course, were in 1933 dollars.) A detailed analysis revealed no significant variations in attendance between the four quarters of the school year, or between the first five years of the plan (1928-33) and the previous five years.[5]

Analyzing the students' academic performance, Vanderslice found that there was no appreciable difference in performance during any of the four quarters, although the October 10-January 15 vacation quarter had the lowest grades. He concluded that "There is no evidence that the four-quarter plan is detrimental to pupil progress in school, and there is no indication that pupil progress in school is hampered by attendance during the warm months of the year."

H. S. Irons, a principal in the Ambridge, Pennsylvania, school system, had less enthusiasm for the plan. He reported that vacation schedules were considered troublesome, that "dropouts" increased, and that considerable administrative reorganization was necessary to handle the complexities of enrolling students at the start of each quarter.[6]

Ultimately, both Aliquippa and Ambridge were able to take advantage of United States Public Works Administration financing for expansion of their building plants. In 1938, both abandoned the year-round plan. When adequate buildings became available, there was no need to enforce calendar reform. In retrospect, it is apparent that the single factor which contributed most to abandonment of the plan was community disaffection. Workers were reluctant to fit their vacation plans to the school's calendar. It was even necessary for Jones & Laughlin, the principal industry in Aliquippa, to bluntly inform parents that they would take their vacations during the three months selected by the public schools, or that they could seek jobs elsewhere.

At Ambridge, another administrator commented, "The plan was extremely difficult to administer; it was unpopular with parents; and it was discontinued as soon as new buildings were completed." It was obvious that in both communities, a sufficient number of parents disliked the inability to take full length summer vacations, and that dissatisfaction with the summer quarter plan was the primary reason for abandonment.

SCHEDULING PROBLEM

Administrative difficulties were compounded because there was no data processing system to take over the complexities of classroom scheduling. There was also evidence of dissatisfaction with a plan that turned one fourth of the students, particularly high school pupils, loose on the streets during all three winter quarters.

Despite the difficulties over vacations and pupil scheduling, Aliquippa and Ambridge were both important historical bench marks in school calendar revision. The programs gave evidence that there was no educational loss to those who took their vacations in the fall, winter, and spring quarters. The programs also demonstrated concrete savings in the cost of operating school buildings—particularly in the area of bond and interest financing.

The conclusions reached in Aliquippa and Ambridge were destined to play an important role in future debates over the pros and cons of year-round school plans. Businessmen and taxpayers tended to focus on the proof of economic savings and the length of the experiments. However, school administrators generally found reasons for opposing the plans followed in the Pennsylvania towns because of evidence of administrative complexities and the opposition of parents.

OMAHA ACCELERATES

Another variation of the four-quarter plan was tried out in the thirties in a large technical high school in Omaha, Nebraska, which had a registration of 4,000 students. Omaha's plan differed from those in Aliquippa and Ambridge in one important respect: the summer quarter was entirely voluntary.[7]

The objectives of the Omaha board of education encompassed both dollar savings and improvement in educational offerings. The theory was that a significant number of students would accelerate through their four years of high school, taking full courses in three summer quarters. There was no attempt to schedule students for fall, winter, and spring quarters. It was hoped, also, that some students would advance to higher levels of apprenticeship through taking additional vocational courses in the summer months.

Dr. Harvey A. Burke, Omaha's superintendent of schools, diagnosed the "failure" of the experiment of the thirties in a monograph submitted to the American Federation of Teachers in 1953.

> The four-quarter plan interfered seriously with the ability of pupils to work during the summer months—a factor which was especially important, because of the socioeconomic level of the neighborhood.
> The four-quarter plan was abandoned because it was not economical, at least as far as operating costs were concerned. Classes were too small; it was difficult to maintain voluntary attendance in summertime, and it was impossible to enforce a compulsory school law during the summer months. There were

no reductions in the maintenance and repair budgets; and, in fact, the latter cost more, because we had to concentrate on the maintenance of a large building for a shorter length of time. We did, however, use a very expensive building more effectively.

Careful analysis revealed that there were no savings, benefits, or advantages accrued to the community, except for the more efficient utilization of space in one building. The plan enabled some students to complete school in three years, but this was at a time when college entrance was not an important factor. It did permit students who had learned a trade or some special skill in school to enter the labor market a year earlier. . . . Pupils, parents and teachers did not consider the plan more effective educationally than the three-quarter plan, except in the savings of time for young people who had learned a trade or skill. . . .

Dr. Burke said that the Omaha administration would not attempt to force young people to attend summer school, because of interference with family life, and that it would not (in 1953) re-instate the plan. The Omaha superintendent said that in 1952 approximately one fourth of the district's secondary school population was enrolled in voluntary summer schools of eight to ten weeks' duration. This enrollment was proportionately larger than that in the technical high school's summer quarters during the thirties.

3

Hiatus

Interest in both compulsory and voluntary year-round school calendar revision lagged in the forties. In Aliquippa and Ambridge, scenes of the two most significant compulsory programs, the need for a mandatory four-quarter plan ended when the federal government made funds available for school building in needy communities through the Roosevelt-sponsored Public Works Administration. This program combined outright grants with federal loans and made a tremendous impact on the expansion of the nation's public school facilities in the late thirties.

Another factor tending to alleviate the pressures of population on the school systems was the relative stability of the birth rate between 1930 and 1940. There had been tremendous pressures to expand schools in the twenties. But there was little pressure in the thirties or the forties.

Financing of home construction under Federal Housing Administration and Veterans Administration home loan insurance programs did not begin on a large scale until the end of World War II. Hence, there was no population "explosion" in the suburbs or in urban centers. The public was still depression conscious, and resisted approval of bond referendums for school construction except where the bill was "sweetened" by the availability of public money.

The entry of the United States into World War II was followed immediately by War Production Board limitations on all construction except for defense-related industries. Few schools were constructed, and these were mostly built in such war-impacted areas as the satellite communities surrounding Army camps, Naval stations, and Air Force bases. Communities used ingenious methods to get on the "priorities list." Glenview, Illinois, for example, built its revolutionary Rugen Elementary School from brick, lumber, and trusses salvaged from an archaic school building that had been torn down to permit extension of the main runway at the nearby Glenview Naval Air Base.

Most overcrowding in schools was alleviated by the inauguration of double shifts; usually one half of the students went to school from 8 a.m. to noon, and the second half from 12:30 to 4:30 p.m. This plan worked a hardship on students, teachers, and parents and was widely regarded as educationally unsound. There was a shortage of teachers, with many male and female teachers giving up the profession to enter higher-paying defense jobs in war plants. Some of the teachers remaining were required to work both shifts—a plan that offered a temporary economic advantage but added to resistance to any doubling up of children.

POSTWAR SCHOOL BUILDING BOOM

With the end of World War II in 1945, the American education system embarked on nearly two decades of rapid expansion. High schools, colleges, and vocational and trade schools were all hit immediately by a flood of enrollments as the United States hastened to disarm. Many young men who had been "dropouts" prior to the draft had become exposed to the sophisticated machinery of war. They had seen first hand how the technical and noncommissioned officer ranks were filled with high school graduates, while many men possessing college degrees ended up with commissions.

There was a rush to complete high school education in both public and private schools and in a rapid proliferation of trade and vocational schools offering to prepare the high school graduates for skilled employment in metalworking, electronics, aviation, and other careers. The students returning from military service were deadly earnest about their education. They felt that they had wasted years in service, and they pressed to complete their school work as early as possible by carrying the maximum number of units offered, and by attending summer sessions. As the result, voluntary summer schools, usually of eight or ten weeks duration, became an accepted part of many public high school programs. Within a few years, educators were to see summer school enrollments add up to a fourth or a third of registrations in winter classes.

The prime motive of most extended secondary school and college programs at the time was acceleration; mature young men wanted to "catch up" and to graduate as early as possible. However, non-veterans and veterans alike registered for both enrichment and review programs. There was no immediate pressure to build a large number of new secondary schools; this pressure was to await the maturing of "war babies" and the children of returning service men. High schools were expanded, largely by the construction of additional classrooms, shops, libraries, gyms, and swimming pools. Financing offered no serious, immediate, nationwide problem. Most high school districts had deferred expansion for five or ten years, because of the war and had the necessary bonding capacity to pay for their urgent additions. Voters, in general, were convinced easily of the necessity for approving the first school building bond referendums. The need was apparent to all.

There was not much thought of school calendar reform at this time. Urgent school "housing" problems were solved by locally financed construction programs, and any desire for extending the school year for reasons of enrichment, acceleration, or remedial needs was offset by the convenient success of what has become the traditional summer school.

GI BILL HITS COLLEGES

The "GI Bill of Rights," and the returning flood of veterans with high school diplomas or partial college credits, had an immediate heavy impact on the entire college and university structure. Pressures, which began with the first returning veterans in 1945, have continued to mount with succeeding generations. Both traditional four-year-graduate universities and the newly discovered public junior and community colleges have embarked on a seemingly endless construction treadmill.

Calendar reform was quick to come at the college-university level. Many traditional institutions had begun four-quarter, three-quarter, and trimester programs even before World War II. Now they expanded, making it possible for the returning GI's to attend classes for eleven months out of the year, and to complete their baccalaureate programs in three years, instead of four. There was little debate over calendar reform. The returning GI's were a serious, "no nonsense" generation, and the colleges accommodated their desires for higher education with additional classrooms, federally financed dormitories and apartments, and practical revision of college calendars to permit the returning veterans to attend school "year round."

The "war baby" population explosion hit the elementary schools in the first of three waves as the decade of the fifties opened. Initially, like the secondary schools, most of the elementary school districts had reserve bonding capacity upon which they could draw to fulfill the urgent elementary school building requirements of the early fifties. The elementary school building boom continued unabated until the late fifties. Through most of this period, voters continued to support building bond referendums with "their hearts." The returning veteran generation was a dominant segment of the electorate; it wanted "the best" in education and school buildings for its children; it had not yet become fully aware of the spiraling cost of all government.

The late forties and the early fifties introduced a new problem to the school building scene. This was the large-scale merchant or operative builder, particularly the erector of prefabricated homes. The younger families, as they were formed, left the central cities for the suburbs. The exodus from older neighborhoods was facilitated by the "GI Bill of Rights," with its provisions for Veterans Administration insurance of long-term, low-down-payment mortgage loans. Skillful home builders were able to "mortgage out" their construction programs, thus enabling thousands of veterans to acquire early post-war housing with "no money down." The Federal Housing Administration, its parent U.S. Department of Housing and Urban Development, and the Federal Home Loan Bank liberalized the terms for conventional mortgages. Ultimately homes were to be financed by these traditional agencies with as little as ten percent down.

In Illinois a few builders, such as Philip Klutznick and Nathan Manilow of Park Forest and Kimball Hill of Rolling Meadows, recognized the importance of schools to the continuation of their booming housing sales. These builders at first turned over homes or apartments to newly expanded local school districts to serve as temporary classrooms. Later they financed the construction of the first elementary and high schools from their operating profits until the school districts gained enough assessed valuation and bonding power to purchase the buildings. Smaller builders simply ignored the problem.

SUBURBAN TAX BURDEN

By the mid-fifties, the tax burden had become the major problem in the suburbs. Churches and hospitals solicited uncommitted funds to provide necessary community facilities. Municipalities built fire stations, village halls, police stations, and elevated water storage tanks. Park districts scrambled to save available land for recreation. And there were schools and more schools. The real devil, of course, was the combination of increased federal taxation with inflation. The total tax burden was more than the typical home owner could bear. But the voter had no voice on the imposition of taxes at state and federal levels; municipal taxes were usually inconsequential. The only way the aroused voter could register his taxation complaint formally and loudly, was by voting "no" at the school referendum. An increasing number of school bond issues and tax-rate proposals was defeated at the polls. School Boards and administrations were forced to turn to new methods for solving school housing problems.

Public school systems that had adopted voluntary summer school programs for their high schools began to explore seriously the possibility of getting greater utilization of their present school buildings through some form of school calendar revision. Optional summer school programs were expanded in a number of cities, financed by payment of tuition, or by newly legislated state aid. The goal of these programs was largely that of educational enrichment. School housing was not a dominant factor. However, a number of cities began to explore some form of year-round school program as a potential solution to the growing problem of over-crowded schools.

San Mateo county, California, studied a four-quarter program in 1951, but concluded that this program had as many disadvantages as the "double-shift" plan. The study committee reported that the four-quarter organization had serious limitations at the elementary level, but that it "has considerable possibilities for application at the high school level, if enthusiastic support is secured from important segments of the community before the plan is put in operation." The four-quarter plan was envisaged as offering "an expanded opportunity for all students to get more schooling during each calendar year." The report concluded, "Such opportunity would add to the cost of education, and ignores the building shortage aspect, which has been primarily responsible for consideration of the plan by California school districts in recent years."

In 1951, Royal Oak, Michigan, put the question of year-round classes up to the voters. Interestingly, 70 percent of the parents said that they favored "year-round school." However, 95 percent of the parents said they did not wish their children to go to school "in the summer." In short, "The idea is fine, but not for me!" The plan was rejected.

In 1954, Dr. Alex J. Stoddard, superintendent of Los Angeles schools, began an "exhaustive study" of the four-quarter plan, as a means for meeting the housing requirements of the city's schools.[1] The study was completed by Dr. Claude L. Reeves, Dr. Stoddard's successor, who said, "I am convinced that the advantages of organizing a school year on a year-round basis are more than offset by the disadvantages." A substantial number of Los Angeles students were then on half-day or split-shift sessions. Their successors still are.

During the same period, the Citizens Study Council of Fairfield, Connecticut, studied a plan that would send children to school for eleven months. The committee held that the plan would have economic advantages, through deferring construction of needed school plant. However, the committee held, the social and administrative disadvantages far outweigh the economic advantages." The plan was rejected.

In 1956, the National Education Association noted "that every school system that has attempted a twelve-month school has later abandoned it, and every community which has thoroughly investigated the plan has rejected it." This situation was destined to hold true for another twelve years.

4

Debate

Interest in extended year and year-round school calendars mounted in the mid-fifties. However, the impetus came from outside the public school systems.

First rumblings of a taxpayer revolt as a catalyst to calendar reform came in 1951, when the Illinois Taxpayers' Federation proposed in an article in the Chicago *Daily News* that the staggered or sequential (Aliquippa) quarter plan be revived. The taxpayers' group was apparently the first in the fifties to look upon year round school programs as a device for making significant savings in the capital cost of school buildings.

Dr. Arthur H. Rice, the distinguished editor of *The Nation's Schools* was quick to seize upon the impact of the proposal. In 1951, he polled his 16,000 school-administrator readers to secure their attitudes on the four-quarter program and other prospective plans for extended school years and year round schools. Fewer than ten percent of the superintendents favored a change in the traditional school calendar.[1] The substantial majority mentioned such objections as administrative and scheduling difficulties, opposition to non-summer vacations, the belief that summertime is not conducive to study, and the belief that teachers need two and three months of summer vacation in order to recoup from the tensions of the winter quarters.

Four years later, in 1955, Dr. Rice repeated his survey of administrator opinion, with little change of results.[2] Of those who replied, 72 percent were distinctly unfavorable to any summer plans. To the former objections, they added the problems of building and classroom maintenance, which is normally conducted by regular custodians during the summer months, when there is no school. They also felt that the savings from increased utilization of buildings would be offset by the higher costs of teachers' salaries and all miscellaneous expenses.

School administrator opinion remained substantially frozen, according to later surveys conducted in the late fifties and early sixties by *School Executive* and *School Management,* also edited for the school administrator audience.

An upsurge of voter demand for relief from mounting school taxes became the dominant public school public relations problem in the mid-fifties. Noble J. Puffer, then Cook County (Illinois) superintendent of schools, called a large downtown Chicago meeting of school administrators and board members in December, 1954, to consider school budget problems. The atmosphere was electric. The meeting was dominated by the representatives of young suburban school districts, which were exhausting their bonding power and were seeking immediate relief. Puffer responded by introducing a number of manufacturers of prefabricated school buildings and demountable classrooms, as well as architects who had achieved especially low initial building costs by sacrificing maintenance-free materials for substitutes that would later bring high maintenance costs. One of Puffer's aides introduced the staggered or sequential four-quarter continuous school year plan as a means of increasing the useful capacity of school buildings by one third. However, he aroused only mild interest from the board members, and none at all from the administrators.

COOLING CARAVAN SELLS

Manufacturers of school ventilating, air conditioning, and temperature control equipment were quick to sense that the "year-round school" idea offered them great sales potential. Charles S. Stock, then marketing manager of American Air Filter Company, Louisville, Kentucky, directed his product engineers to rush development of summer air-conditioning equipment designed especially for classroom use. Then he sent what he called "A Cooling Caravan" on a tour of 52 northern and southern cities. More than 3,000 school administrators, architects, and School Board members attended luncheon and dinner meetings at which they viewed a motion picture, "For Better Schooling—Cooling," and looked over classroom unit ventilators that were designed for "future cooling." Within one year, Stock reported, American Air Filter Company had sold more than $3 million worth of "future cooling" ventilators, which had piping and coils for cooling, but no refrigeration units. And the firm's total sales of ventilation equipment to schools increased more than 25 percent. Minneapolis-Honeywell Company, Trane, Nesbitt, Chromalox, and Lennox all climbed on the bandwagon, successfully introducing summer air conditioning into the plans for hundreds of schools to be built during the next decade. But school calendars remained unchanged.

The idea of year-round schools caught on quickly with taxpayers' associations and chambers of commerce, which were swayed readily by the arguments that school plants were "lying idle" three months out of the year, and that the traditional long summer vacation was wasting the taxpayers' money. Many of these associations, especially the Illinois State Chamber of Commerce, offered compelling arguments for using school buildings in the summer months, and carried their campaigns directly to School Board members, administrators, and parents. However, most of the advocates of year-round schools were vague about the specifics and educational implications of their proposals. School administrators were largely unmoved by the pressures and were responsive to the arguments of teachers who were solidly behind the traditional 180-day school year.

THE BEEP OF SPUTNIK

A powerful new voice joined the debate on October 5, 1957. It was the "beep" of Sputnik, Russia's first orbiting satellite which weighed only 183.6 pounds but was destined to shake the scientific and educational thinking of the world. Later, sober minds were to realize that Russia's success in launching the first satellite was due to political and military decisions and not to any great lead in science. (In fact, both the Russian and American space programs were dominated by captured German scientists and engineers.) But the message was obvious, Russia was emerging from the "dark ages" and was challenging the scientific and educational leadership of the United States.

United States politicians, businessmen, and many educators turned to a searching examination of the entire U.S. educational structure, from the elementary schools through the graduate technical schools of the great universities. Chief target was the teaching of the physical

sciences and mathematics. The public readily accepted the thesis that
our schools and colleges had been asleep and that they had been
surpassed by their Soviet counterparts. The public demanded, and
got, a complete overhaul of the teaching of sciences and mathematics. Suddenly, chemistry and physics, which had been considered
"difficult subjects" in high school and college, became important
parts of the general science program in junior high schools. The
teaching of algebra penetrated from the eleventh grade to the sixth
grade.

School curricula at all levels were expanded to accommodate the
"information explosion" that was taking place. The Congress passed,
and President Eisenhower signed, The National Defense Education
Act of 1958, which infused the entire educational structure of the
nation with funds for innovations and equipment and learning resources. The "information explosion" argument brought with it a
revival of demands for a longer school year to permit students "to
keep up with the world's rapidly growing technology."

The authors question the validity of the "information explosion
argument." They believe the role of elementary education is to help
children acquire learning skills and critical judgment; to arouse their
interest in a lifetime of learning in which they will constantly improve their working skills and relationships with society. To the authors, education is not the acquisition of a conglomeration of mem-
orized "facts" or content materials, to be forgotten in later life. They
do realize, however, that thy "great debate" over education served a
useful purpose in arousing self examination of the educational structure, and all aspects of curriculum, administration, and operations.

The debate over education set off a new debate over the traditional nine-month or ten-month school calendar that was to continue
unabated for the next thirteen years and shows no sign of tapering
off. A bibliography prepared by the Utica Community Schools,
Utica, Michigan, in 1970, lists more than 400 articles on the "year-
round school" published in professional and business journals and in
national magazines edited for the public. Many newspapers added
their voices to the rising demand for calendar reform, although few
of the writers were certain whether they were arguing for an extended school year or for some form of rotation that would get
greater mileage out of school buildings. The roster of publications
climbing on the "year-round school" bandwagon included *Parents,
Good Housekeeping, Ladies Home Journal, McCall's* and *Saturday*

Review.[3] Even the powerful *Reader's Digest* entered the argument with an expose of the "lavish extravagance" in closing school buildings for the summer hiatus that was published first in 1959[4] and was then repeated with an article by a second writer in 1966.[5] The barrage of general publicity had its impact on School Boards and on administrators, who began a mounting chain of feasibility studies, conferences, and legislative lobbying that added to the fuel of debate over assorted year-round school plans.

ADMINISTRATORS SOFTEN

One result of the mounting publicity given year-round school proposals was a noticeable change in the attitudes of school administrators towards school calendar revision. *Nation's Schools,* in 1958, conducted another of its series of opinion studies on the subject and noted this time that two thirds of the respondents were opposed to lengthening or otherwise changing the school year, while the number of those favorable to change had increased to 33 percent.

The well-known education commentators, Grace and Fred Hechinger, writing in the *New York Times Magazine* in 1960, labeled the traditional nine-month school year as a "relic of the past." They said, schools will cease placing barriers before children who want, for whatever reason, to attend school during the summer.

Most of the discussion continued to be about extended school year plans that offered students more days or more hours of classtime. Some discussions, however, centered about various plans for staggering the school year, so as to increase the number of students who might be accommodated in any school building. The Illinois legislature, in 1961, passed the first of three revisions of its school code, designed to permit "three-quarter" plans or an "extended year" plan of 235 days, thus neatly straddling the subject, opening schools to consideration of plans designed for either economic reasons, or for enrichment. However, it was to be nine years before any Illinois school system actually undertook a major revision of the school calendar.

One of the most comprehensive studies of the economic feasibility of calendar revision for economic reasons was undertaken by the Board of Education of Montgomery County, Maryland, a largely suburban district impacted by the growth of the federal government. The Montgomery report took note of the prediction that the number of school-age children in the county would increase from 80,000 to 106,000 in the five-year period ending June 30, 1966—an increase of a little more than one fourth. Facing "the urgent need for accommodating 5,000 to 6,000 more students each year," the superintendent of schools concluded that operation of the schools year round would help solve the schools' housing problem, as well as *improve instruction.* The administration proposed a "twelve-four" plan—a calendar calling for twelve weeks of classes followed by a four-week vacation. The classes were to be staggered so that one fourth of the students would be on vacation, and three fourths of the students in school, at any given time. This was essentially a "semantic" variation of the nine-month, three-month plan that had been followed in Aliquippa and Ambridge, Pennsylvania, in the thirties. The report noted that a building with a capacity of 600 pupils could thus accommodate 800 in the course of a school year, under the staggered plan. Turning to economic feasibility, the Montgomery administration estimated that construction of sufficient extra buildings to house the 26,000 additional students expected would cost $13 million a year, or approximately $62 million in all. In contrast, the Montgomery administration estimated that the existing buildings could be air conditioned at a total cost of $4 million, and that the operating cost of cooling would be approximately $700,000 annually.

Montgomery's superintendent of schools made a good case for the educational advantages of school calendar revision. He said that the quality of education would be improved through initial grouping by age; more prompt recognition of abilities; opportunity for remedial or disciplinary action as needed; and greater flexibility in handling special problems. The superintendent noted that special handling could be provided for gifted children. He also argued that the overall achievement of the pupils would be increased due to the shorter vacation periods, thus "lessening" the "forgetting" which occurs during the summer months. He indicated that classes could be smaller and more flexible and that double sessions could be eliminated.

The Montgomery report, however, noted a number of disadvantages, which are essentially those that have killed consideration of four-quarter calendar plans in other school systems. These include difficulties in matching vacation periods for children and parents, difficulties of taking long summer vacation trips, and problems of interscholastic sports scheduling and building maintenance. The report predicted that clerical, administrative, supervisory, and maintenance needs would increase, and that there would be difficulty identifying which children on the playground were "attending school," and which were "on vacation." The report also expressed difficulty in matching enrollments for the four quarters—one of the problems which arose at Ambridge—where parents resented arbitrary assignments to fall, winter and spring vacations for their children. In the last analysis, the Montgomery county board found that the disadvantages outweighed the advantages—at least for the twelve-four plan—and the proposed plan was never implemented.

Dr. George Gallup in a newspaper poll in 1961 asked parents to comment on plans for increasing the school year. Seventy percent of parents of elementary school children polled by Gallup's interviewers were opposed to a longer school year; 26 percent were in favor; and four percent had no opinion. Sixty-four percent of high school parents opposed a longer school year; 26 percent were in favor; and five percent had no opinion.

In January, 1962, the prestigious National Education Association published a report on the "All Year School," listing pros and cons, but taking no position for calendar reform. The U.S. Office of Education wrote a report on the "All Year School" the same year, and Tucson, Arizona, focused on a five-term plan, but took no action. In the fall of 1962, the Department of Education of Florida State University, Tallahassee, began a pilot study of a 225-day school year, organized into trimesters of 75 days each. The plan embraced students at all primary and high school levels, and was linked with a nongraded organization and curriculum. The plan was dropped in 1967.

NOVA HIGH EXPERIMENTS

Concurrently, the innovative Nova High School in Fort Lauderdale, Florida, experimented with a similar 220-day trimester school year, which was also linked to a nongraded program.[6] The nongraded plan permitted 10th grade students entering the three-year institution to progress at their own individual rates through a series of achievement levels in each subject. Under this nongraded plan, a beginning 10th grader could complete his three year graduation requirements in two and one-third years. Nova's program was discontinued in 1965 for several reasons, namely "a strain on students and teachers, caused by a lack of vacations"; a psychological "let-down" among students who had to stay in school for seven weeks while their playmates were on vacation; pressure from parents to have their children released for July vacations; and other problems concerning faculty budget and certification of teachers. It was re-vived later.

There was evidence, however, of rapid growth in summer school "enrichment" programs. In 1962, Michigan State University's Educa-tional Research service found one fifth of the schools with summer school programs had initiated them since 1958. The surveyors found that 68 percent of the elementary summer school systems offered remedial work, 56 percent offered enrichment, and 40 percent of-fered "make-up" work. At junior high, 56 percent offered make-up and remedial work, while 60 percent offered enrichment courses. In senior high, 90 percent listed make-up opportunities, and 75 percent listed remedial work. The majority of the systems offered summer school work for both elementary and high school students. A "signif-icant number" permitted students to take summer work to speed up graduation.

The California Elementary School Administrators Association, late in 1965, conducted a survey of parent attitudes on a staggered four-quarter plan, finding that 75 percent of the parents responded nega-tively. The following year California's legislature appropriated $145,000 to conduct a pilot study of a nine-month, three-month staggered school plan in Del Campo High School, near Sacramento. The first quarter was scheduled for May, 1966, but was delayed a year due to a lack of interest among students and parents. In the fall of the same year, the Del Campo High School Board of Education decided to drop the program, citing "a lack of funds, student disin-terest, and parental apathy."

During the next five years from a dozen to a score of school districts in every part of the country were destined to conduct stud-ies of various year-round programs in varying depth. Pilot studies were begun in several places, notably in New York State. However, the weight of administrative, board and parental opinion continued to affect adversely the serious implementation of any extended year programs, except in two school districts, which will be dealt with in the following chapter, on "Framework."

In this chapter on "Debate," the authors have quoted at random from the highlights of a file drawer full of printed reports and surveys of "year round school" plans, which have been accumulated during the three years since the Valley View Public Schools (District 96 of Will County, Illinois) began to study seriously the implementation of a calendar revision program in the district. It is interesting to note that more than a score of specific calendars has been proposed. It is also interesting to note that many commentators have failed to make a clear distinction between plans concerned with more efficient utilization of school buildings and those concerned with offering students opportunities for educational enrichment, make-up, or remedial work. The authors believe that enrichment plans should be distinguished clearly from "building utilization" plans, which have goals primarily economic. This does not mean that a plan for rotating different groups of students in the use of school buildings at different times does not have educational advantages. The Montgomery county, Maryland, report indicated intrigue with the possibility that students might reduce the traditional summer "learning lag" or hiatus by having shorter vacations, and the possibility that the weeks out of school might be used effectively for make-up work or enrichment programs. These subjects will be covered later in the book, in the chapters concerned specifically with the Valley View schools.

COOK COUNTY CLARIFIES

The very variety of comment, study, and report that the authors have brought to the reader thus far may be somewhat confusing and may not bear on his specific school administration problems or goals. With this problem in mind, the authors at this point have digested and quote at considerable length from a report prepared in February, 1968, by Roy A. Wehmhoefer, assistant superintendent in the Office of the Cook County Superintendent of Schools, in Chicago, Illinois.[7] Wehmhoefer's analysis of the "possibility of avoiding building programs by staggering the enrollment over the school year" is one of the best we have seen, and summarizes clearly the pros and cons for the reader.

Wehmhoefer noted in his introduction that most of the inquiries received by Robert P. Hanrahan, Cook County Superintendent of Schools, came from people "concerned with increasing school enrollments, and with reorganization of the school year to avoid building programs." The Cook County report is, therefore, concerned with one aspect of year-round schools, the four-quarter system with rotating attendance. Wehmoefer clearly separates the different potential meanings of "year-round schools" into five categories:

1. Operation of the schools on a four-quarter system with rotating attendance.

2. Operation of the schools throughout the year.

3. Summer school to supplement the regular school year for make-up work, acceleration, enrichment, camps, and recreation programs.

4. An extended service term for teachers, with emphasis on in-service growth and school improvement activities.

5. Any variations or combinations of the above types.

The quarter plan, as referred to by Wehmhoefer, "usually means dividing a year equally into four periods, with approximately 75 percent of the student body attending in any one period. Teachers could be employed for an entire year, nine months, or shorter periods of time mutually agreed upon by the teacher and the school board." Wehmhoefer lists the advantages of the four-quarter plan as follows:

1. Utilization of buildings. A district could increase from an enrollment of 3,000 students to 4,000 students, with only three fourths of the students in the buildings at any one time.

2. Need for fewer teachers. A staff of 75 teachers could be paid the same total salaries as a staff of 100 under conventional scheduling, greatly enhancing teachers' earnings.

3. Enhancement of economic status of teachers. A teacher could practice his profession "full time" instead of seeking less remunerative summer employment.

4. Improvement of educational program. Teachers released from classroom duties could participate in in-service training workshops, curriculum development work, research, substitute teaching, and tutorial service.

5. Alleviation of teacher shortage. Employment of teachers not fully qualified could be eliminated.

6. Need for fewer textbooks. Texts would be needed for only 75 percent of total enrollment because of fuller utilization.

7. Better utilization of library materials and equipment. One fourth fewer students would demand a given supply of books and equipment at any given time.

8. Guidance counselor ratio reduction. One counselor's load could be cut from 500 students to 375 students during any given quarter.

9. Children entering school at a time closest to legal age of en-

trance. No need for December children to wait until the following September, thus eliminating one of the principal reasons for the wide range of maturity and ability in the typical primary grade.

10. Year-round vacation schedules for business and industry.

11. Greater employment opportunities for youths, with fewer in the job market at one time. Industry could also have student employees the year round.

12. Teachers attendance at regular sessions of educational colleges, instead of summer sessions.

13. Shortening or modification of courses. They could be converted into quarter units, instead of semester units.

14. Facilitation of acceleration or retention of students for make-up work by change to quarter courses.

Although Wehmhoefer lists many good arguments for the four-quarter school system, he also finds formidable disadvantages. Some of these are:

1. Increased educational cost. Raises would push up faculty salaries, which make up from 75 to 85 percent of the typical school budget.

2. Increased maintenance costs. The loss of annual vacation maintenance time would require hiring of extra custodians for the few vacation weeks that are open in the schedule.

3. No increase in state aid. (The Illinois Legislature has remedied this problem by passage of special legislation fostering twelve-month schools, and authorizing the State Superintendent of Public Instruction to take into account all four student groups in computing state aid on an average daily attendance basis.)

4. Large enrollments needed. An elementary school, for example, would need a school population of 720 to permit formation of four groups of students. A junior high would need 1,500.

5. Certain times undesirable for vacation. (Here, of course, is the back-breaking argument on which most attempts to initiate a nine-month, three-month system have foundered.)

6. Quarterly entrance creating problems for both school and parent. Suppose a parent had children born in four different quarters? And, the distribution of births by quarters is unequal. Due to the prevalence of June weddings and conceptions, the February-April quarter has 45 percent more birthdays than the May-July quarter.

7. Increase in truancy. Children out of school would tempt those in school.

8. Transfer problems. Students would be set back as much as a

semester, when they moved into a district with a traditional school calendar.

9. Hampering of extra-curricular activities and interscholastic sports. It is needless to point out that all of the members of the high school football squad would have to be in school for the fall quarter.

10. Teacher recruitment. Teachers are looking for jobs that begin in September, and it would be difficult to recruit for jobs that start in other quarters.

To this formidable list of disadvantages, Wehmhoefer added the inflexibility of school codes. Fortunately, spurred by the problems of Valley View District 96, and the support of the Illinois State Chamber of Commerce, the Illinois School Code was amended in 1968, 1969, and 1970 to remove most, if not all, the obstacles to school calendar revision.

In summary, the authors note that almost every proposal for a four-quarter school plan has met with defeat for several over-riding reasons:

1. Parents simply will not accept a three month vacation in midwinter. What northern school superintendent could hope to overcome the aroused opposition of mothers who would be forced to let their children spend their only prolonged vacation time in ice, snow, mud, and slush?

2. Administrative problems seem formidable, but not insurmountable. These include scheduling of students in classes, scheduling maintenance, and selling teachers on the plan.

3. There is just plain inertia. The pattern of three-month summer vacations, summer jobs, and attendance at summer teacher colleges for advanced degree work are parts of the American school scene that teachers and administrators are reluctant to change.

In the opinion of the authors, the three-month midwinter vacation is the most formidable obstacle to any staggered four-quarter plan. It is an interesting commentary on the state of American school administration that scores of administrators, whose districts really needed some form of staggered year-round school, stopped short when they encountered this obstacle. Obviously, very few had the initiative to explore for alternative plans that would spread out the midwinter vacation period over other seasons.

It is noteworthy that the two midwest school systems whose administrators explored beyond the staggered four-quarter calendar plan, and developed viable alternatives, had no difficulty with disposing of all of the other disadvantages that Wehmhoefer has cataloged.

5

Framework

The "sixties" proved to be fruitful years in expansion and development of year-round school ideas, although no school systems were to undertake broad, significant steps in calendar revision until the end of the decade.

The principal manifestation of progress in school calendar revision was in enabling state legislation. Illinois, early in the sixties, passed an act authorizing the State Superintendent of Public Instruction to permit rotation of vacation quarters, providing that a school system maintained a minimum of 180 days of instruction. No Illinois schools adopted any of the eligible plans, however.

In 1963, the New York State Joint Legislative Committee on School Financing recommended a study of the educational feasibility and the sociological and psychological implications of a rescheduling of the school year. The continuing study was assigned to the State Education Department, also known as the University of the State of New York.[1] Interestingly, the study program the department entered upon was under the general direction of James E. Allen, Jr., Commissioner of Education, who was later to become President Nixon's first Commissioner of Education in the U.S. Department of Health, Education and Welfare, and an active proponent of calendar revision.

The directive from the New York Joint Legislative Committee was explicit. Its objective was "to effect a possible saving of one, *or even two,* years" in the traditional thirteen years of elementary and secondary schooling. The main thrust of the New York research, therefore, was acceleration. The goal was to find ways of getting each child to accomplish more days of schooling each year, thus progressing bit by bit through his eighth or thirteenth year of schooling in earlier years, and turning him out of the school system one or two years earlier than he might be graduated under traditional calendars. The arithmetic behind the idea was simple. If a student could accomplish his eighth year of elementary schooling at the end of the seventh year, there would be approximately one eighth fewer students in the school system after the first group had progressed to graduation, thus increasing the number of available classroom seats by a corresponding ratio. The idea of shortening the combined years of elementary and high school education by two years was even more attractive to the legislators. This might free one sixth of all the seats and classrooms in New York State, and thus save more than $300 million of school construction costs over approximately a dozen school years.

GEORGE ISAIAH THOMAS, APOSTLE

In 1964, Commissioner Allen assigned George Isaiah Thomas, an educator with a missionary zeal for calendar reform, to the post of Consultant on Rescheduling the School Year, in the Office of Research and Evaluation in the State Education Department. During the past seven years, Thomas aggressively explored every facet of school-year planning, working out in detail a dozen or more programs for accelerating the progress of students through the elementary and high school years. These plans were all lumped under the general heading of "Extended School Year Programs."

Thomas' principal plans, developed during his first three years of research were:

The continuous school year plan
The trimester plan
The quadrimester plan
The modified summer school plan
The extended K to 12 plan.

Thomas dismissed the idea of lengthening the school day, because it would require children in rural New York to leave home at 7 a.m. and return at 4:30 or 5 p.m., with homework to do. He did favor lengthening high school hours to permit more study time in school and to reduce homework at night.

Thomas emphatically favored lengthening the school year from 180 days to 204 or 210, citing the longer school years common in several European countries and the studies completed in Newark, New Jersey, and Nashville, Tennessee, which found that students suffered no ill effect from summer classes. He was careful to broaden the scope of his studies beyond the mere economic savings of the extended school year, urging schools to modify their curricula in order to broaden courses of study and to enrich the entire curriculum. He was also critical of the "staggered quarter" systems that had been developed in Ambridge and Aliquippa, Pennsylvania, because these did not increase the now standard 180-day school year.

Before entering into a description of Thomas' plans, the authors wish to make clear that they do not agree with the premise upon which the New York State Joint Legislative Committee based its entire program. This premise runs counter to all progress in United States education as it has developed over the past 125 years. Most educators and parents will question whether a child is mentally, psychologically, physically, and socially mature enough to leave high school at the age of fifteen or sixteen, instead of seventeen, to then enter college or the work force. In the thirties Robert Maynard Hutchins, then Chancellor of the University of Chicago, conducted an interesting experiment in which exceptional students were force-fed the high school curriculum in their earliest teens and were accepted as freshmen at the University at the ages of thirteen, fourteen, and fifteen. Many exceptional children were, of course, able to cope with the content of Chicago's curriculum in the humanities and sciences. Dr. Hutchins made a good case for his plan. But, upon his departure, the accelerated program for young undergraduates was abandoned.

Despite the legislative restraints under which Thomas has labored over the years, much useful research has been accomplished under his direction. And the smorgasbord of plans he has proposed has been useful to other school administrators who have sought to reform their calendars, whether for economic or educational reasons, or both. For detailed presentation of the various New York plans, the student of school calendar reform can turn to *Extended School Year Designs: An Introduction to Plans for Rescheduling the School Year,* published in January, 1966, by the Office of Research and Evaluation, The State Education Department, Albany, New York 12224.[2]

EXTENDED YEAR PLANS

The principal New York extended year plans, as applied to the 1966-67 school year, are:

1. The trimester plan. School runs from about August 18 or 23 through June 30. The second trimester starts approximately December 5, and the third about March 27. Regular Christmas and spring recess is accommodated in the second trimester. The summers are left free for six or seven weeks of summer vacation, camp, recreation, and travel. The school year totals from 207 to 210 days.

2. The quadrimester plan. School runs from about September 1 through July 21. Quadrimesters begin on November 18, February 13, and May 8. Traditional Christmas and spring recesses are preserved, and the total number of days in school is increased to 212.

3. Modified summer school plan. The regular school year would run from September 6 through June 16, accomplishing a schedule of 183 or 184 days. This would be complemented by a modified summer session from June 19 through August 10, accomplishing 37 classroom days, for a total of 220 to 221 school days in the school year.

The modified summer plan, according to Thomas, is designed to "deliberately accelerate" pupils through secondary school. The purpose is to allow them to take from four to six years of secondary school in one year less. Variations of these plans include the split trimester, which would make 36 days of summer school optional. However, Thomas wrestles with the advisability of optional extended year programs, holding that they will tend to work against disadvantaged students.

In concluding Extended Year Designs, Thomas makes his case on the question of maturity, admitting that the individual's readiness to face life's problems depends upon a combination of inherited factors and acquired experiences. He questions whether an additional year of schooling will perceptibly change the individual's approach to new problems acquired in marriage, college, the army, or working for a living. He points out that increments in physical size are relatively small after a person reaches sixteen years. He contends, also, with some merit, that new techniques in teaching the subjects of mathematics and social sciences, for example, are already carrying high school students into what used to be considered college levels of study. He claims that years of schooling are not necessarily related to maturity, pointing to the fact that there may be a range of five or six years in the achievement levels of students registered in a single grade. He emphasizes, also that remaining an additional year in high school may not be as stimulating as going on to a community college or a vocational school. Educators can debate the "maturity" issue for years to come. The authors believe, despite Thomas' arguments, that the present sixteen-year school plan, followed universally in the United States, takes into account the normal physical, mental, psychological, and sociological growth of children. It is doubtful whether the voters of New York, or any other state, will be willing to turn children out from school a year younger, just to achieve a calculated increase in the space available in the state's schools.

During the last five years of the sixties, Thomas and his staff have worked with a number of New York State public school systems to field test various aspects of extended school year plans.

In Commack, approximately 1,400 children in grades one through six attended four elementary schools from August through June. The pupils were able to complete normal grade requirements at various times during the lengthened school year, which was not divided into trimesters or quadrimesters, and to move ahead to work planned normally for the next year's curriculum. Here the extended school year totaled 210 days. In the Casto-Meridian district, a modified quadrimester school program was introduced in grades kindergarten through six of a central school. The day was lengthened and the year lengthened slightly to achieve the equivalent of 220 to 225 school days.

Syosset experimented with an extended summer segment, in which junior high school students in seventh grade were able to complete the regular eighth grade math course by the end of the summer session, and to move directly into high school algebra. The students were programmed ultimately into an ungraded math program which extended through the ninth, tenth, and twelfth years. The Syosset experiment demonstrated that program content can be "compacted," without harm to the students. However, as the program progressed, a number of volunteer participants dropped out of the accelerated program and returned to the regular schedule. No economic benefits were accomplished.

At Hornell, the administration experimented with a program that would enable high school students to complete a year's study in one subject during seven weeks of longer classes during the summer.[4] The program appealed to "overage" students, who were able to offset their tardy progress through classes. However, voluntary participation lagged. The Hornell experience confirmed that of Syosset—that voluntary programs are destined to failure and that mandatory programs are needed to effect any measurable effect on utilization of buildings.

New York State also tested the utilization of a computer to effect more efficient scheduling of students in a large high school, New York City's Christopher Columbus High School, which was supporting a student population of 4,800 in a building designed for 3,000. The principal gain was that administrators worked out a complex scheduling plan in a few days, which might have taken weeks to accomplish manually. Computers were also applied to modular scheduling in intermediate schools in New York City. The goal here —to break up block schedules or homogeneous grouping and to facilitate grouping students by special needs, by special interests and by sex—was successful. Hilton High School, in 1968, used the computer to work out an application of Thomas' "Multiple Trails" plan—a "modular" or "open scheduling" concept, which theoretically frees up teacher time and classroom space, giving students freedom to pursue individual study through utilization of learning center materials. Students started in August and worked through June, and were mainly able to accomplish additional elective studies.

NO PHYSICAL, EMOTIONAL BARRIERS

The series of tests in New York State schools was designed primarily to determine whether children are able to work successfully in an extended school year program. Thomas states unequivocally that "The research studies show that children can actively participate in a lengthened school year program without harm to them physically, emotionally, socially, and academically." He mentions that Commack children were so enchanted with their summer sessions that they enlisted an additional dozen volunteers for the program after it had started. He states also that students in the New York State extended school year programs "showed no ill effects from a lengthened school year." Individual student attendance records, over four years of experiment, failed to show any drop from the winter level. According to Thomas, extended school year teachers said that they had to cope with fewer emotional problems during the summer sessions than they did during the regular year. One reason, they theorized, was that they had to contend with fewer failures. Another was that they no longer had to spend long weeks in the fall reteaching the previous spring's work. "Students can move into new learning activities without being exposed to the frustration of repetitive review and reteaching when school resumes in the fall," Thomas explains. Some teachers reported a "dramatic reduction" in the emotional regression of students "who were formerly unapproachable when they returned to school in the fall." There were also positive conclusions on the questions of discipline and social development of students, many of whom found their summers "aimless" when they were not in school. In summary, Thomas reported on the test programs, "Learning does not stop with the arrival of the summer solstice. Children and teachers may be a bit uncomfortable when they work in July or August, but their performance or academic growth is as good, if not better, than that of comparable peermates working in fall, winter, and spring terms."

The authors of this book feel Thomas is being influenced here by his marked enthusiasm for the extended school year, making assumptions that are not wholly justified because of one cardinal fact. The various New York State programs upon which he bases his conclusions were mostly voluntary, not mandatory. Thus, in the authors' opinion, there is a possibility that the children who were in attendance in summer sessions represent a biased sample of the more privileged and better students.

With this possible bias in mind, there may be significant clues for the administrator or board member evaluating a possible year-round school program in the results of achievement tests conducted under the aegis of the New York State Department of Education.

Commack conducted reading tests in November among third grade students. After 3.7 months of an extended year program, these students showed a mean gain of 6.5 months in reading comprehension. The third grade median at Commack was eight months higher than that of a control group, and one year above the national norm. A significant conclusion of the Commack tests was that the "slow learner" group made greater gains over its control group than did the average and high groups.*

*Commack is a relatively affluent exurban community in central Long Island. Hence, the comparisons between the control group and the test group may be more valid than those against the national average.

In the Cato-Meridian schools, researchers found that extended school year students made their greatest gain in work study skills such as map reading, reading of graphs and tables, and use of reference materials. This finding, interestingly, parallels another study made by Donald L. Beggs, Assistant Professor, Department of Guidance and Educational Psychology, Southern Illinois University, Carbondale.[5] Professor Beggs tested a group of Iowa public school students on "basic skills." Although he found a distinct lag in some areas during the summer hiatus, there was a marked improvement in vocabulary, map reading, and reading of graphs and tables. Apparently students can acquire some important skills, even though they are not in school during the summer.

Further test in New York State schools by the State Department of Education tended to demonstrate that students attending school in the summer quarter performed at least as well as those completing the same curricular matter during the regular ten months school year.

FOUR QUARTERS "IMPOSSIBLE"

Thomas concludes his March, 1970, study on "The Impact of A Rescheduled School Year" with a series of recommendations to the New York Legislature. He suggests that individual school systems be given power to implement one of the several school plans that he proposes, but specifically objects to the nine-month, three-month staggered four quarter plan as "impossible to sell to the public." He recommends a change in calculation of state aid, similar to that already adopted in Illinois. He suggests state financial aid to those districts offering more than 200 days of class a year, to assist in their adjustment to the extended school year. He opts for a series of currently timely educational innovations, none of which is necessarily related to calendar revision. He also, for the first time, expresses interest in "continuous learning year cycling plans," of which Valley View's 45-15 continuous school year plan is representative. Acceptance of this plan, which is based primarily on the traditional 180-day school year, is a radical departure from the initial directive from the New York Legislative Committee to investigate means of getting children through school at an earlier age. Later in 1970, Mr. Thomas published a brief folder, "What is the Continuous Learning Year Cycling Plan?" In this folder, the New York educational researcher suggests alternating eight weeks in class with two weeks' vacation, a proposal related somewhat to the 45-15 day plan. He points out the potential savings in construction of classroom space, and in transportation, thus accepting in principle the continuous school year plan.[6]

OVERSTUDY TORPEDOES LOUISVILLE PLAN

School systems interested in working out extended school year or continuous school year plans may gain some practical guidance from more than a decade of study by the schools of Jefferson County, Kentucky, which embraces Louisville and most of its suburbs. Jefferson County had explored various year-round school plans since 1955, when a local air conditioning manufacturer, American Air Filter Company, proposed the institution of summer schools as a device to help minimize expenditures for new construction. By September, 1968, the Jefferson County schools' housing plight became so acute that a comprehensive study of various year round school proposals was launched.[7]

The school system followed a "classic approach" to public relations, according to Dr. Oz Johnson, assistant superintendent in charge of the study, with mixed success. The study was "kicked off" with a press conference, which accomplished a great deal of publicity, but tended to "polarize" the community's attitudes on calendar revision. People "froze" their opinions before they had adequate information on the goals and methods of instituting an extended year plan.

Three advisory committees were appointed:

1. A citizens advisory committee charged with examining five extended year plans, with checking the pulse of the community, and with isolating one plan, which would be turned over to an "organizational" committee for detailed study.

2. An organizational committee composed of teachers, principals, supervisors and directors, charged with making sure that any plan adopted would be feasible.

3. A curriculum committee, composed of teachers, an associate superintendent and the director of curriculum. This committee was expected to develop "desired curriculum innovations" better to fulfill the needs of children and the demand of the community.

Because partial information released at the time of the initial press conference had already polarized community opposition to the plan, Dr. Johnson plunged quickly into writing an informational brochure,

"Signs of the Times." This brochure spelled out clearly the things the school system did not intend to do. It explained that the system would not be implemented county-wide until it had been tested in a single district or single school situation. It said that any implementation would be deferred until the 1970-71 school year and would be contingent on widespread community support. In addition to explaining five extended year plans under consideration, it enclosed a questionnaire designed to measure community opinion.

RESISTANCE POLARIZES

Dr. Johnson summarizes the community response as polarized around five objections:

1. That an extended school year would lead to graduation of students at the age of sixteen, making them eligible to move too quickly into the "revolutionary element" current on college campuses.

2. That the plan was being "rammed down the throats" of the members of the public, without adequate citizen involvement.

3. That family vacation schedules would be interrupted.

4. That different school calendars would exist within a single family.

5. That the extended school year would place "too much pressure on the school children."

Replies to more than a thousand questionnaires returned by April 2, 1969, were interesting: Some 52 percent agreed that the schools should be used in the summer months; however, 60 percent voted that they would not want their own children to participate in an extended school year program.

Once again—use of the schools in the summer month makes sense, but for someone else's children.

Half of the respondents said that they did not need more information on which to base their decisions on year round schools. But 74 percent said they would like to hear the subject discussed at PTA and service club meetings.

Questioned about preference for various plans under consideration, 60 percent favored none, or gave no answer. Fifteen percent preferred a "12-4" plan, and ten percent supported a modified summer school plan.

Although discouraged by community reaction, the administrators of the Jefferson County schools have continued to mount a public relations campaign designed to inform the community on the desirability of the proposed pilot project in calendar revision. Dr. Johnson concludes that the "goodness" or "badness" of the extended school year concept lies in the degree of its acceptability by the citizens of the school district. "The development of a truly feasible plan can be accomplished only by giving the most astute consideration to the reactions and feelings of school district pupils, parents and patrons." At the present time the Jefferson county plan is inactive.

GREATER ATLANTA MOVES

Schools in Fulton County, Georgia, which lies largely in the suburban portion of the Atlanta metropolitan area, took a significant step in re-ordering their school calendar in 1968.

Reid Gillis of the Fulton County schools emphasizes that the plan implemented in the Atlanta area has one over-riding purpose—to improve the educational opportunities of children. "It is not designed to save money, to save space, or to use the school buildings year round," Gillis reported to a seminar on year-round education held in Fayetteville, Arkansas, in 1968.

"In our area, we found about 25 percent of our high school enrollment attended summer school. This summer school was an appendix eight weeks long, attached to the regular nine months school year. This program was developed initially for the student who failed, and needed to repeat a course. However, we found that of the 25 percent who attended summer school, 70 percent were taking new work. Also, we found out that there was another group who could not go to summer school because the new course offerings in the existing summer session were not inviting. Therefore, we saw a need for a program in which courses could be taken during any quarter, and have the same integrity, character and quality as any other quarter. This was one point that led us to the four-quarter plan."

The Fulton County schools set up their calendar with four equal quarters, three of which were required, and the fourth optional. Any three of the four quarters will meet Georgia state attendance requirements. Under what Fulton County schools call the "attendance option," students may choose any three of the four quarters, or they may take courses in all four. To graduate from high school (here grades eight through twelve), and to complete college entrance requirements, a student must attend at least three quarters for each of five years. If the student wishes to go to school for four quarters, he may graduate at least one year early, or he may elect 32 quarter courses more than normally required. In commenting on this plan, Mr. Gillis said, "It really doesn't matter when a kid is in school. What does make a difference is the education, and the opportunity the student gets when he comes to school. . . . This new scheduling procedure is only a vehicle to put into operation a new curricular concept, a quarter curriculum in which the child is the center."[8]

CARNEGIE UNIT DROPPED

Fulton County schools have literally thrown out the Carnegie Unit. Totally new courses have been developed on a quarter basis, under which each course terminates at the end of the quarter, and may be taken independently, without regard for sequence, whenever this is possible. Of the courses offered, 70 percent are independent of sequence. For example, a student does not schedule a full year of English; instead he schedules a new course each quarter. If he fails, he may repeat, or he may take another course that fits his needs better. It is no longer necessary for a student to complete a year's work in sequence. Instead, the student gets five hours of credit for each quarter course completed, and must complete 375 credits to graduate.

In English, for example, there are 50 courses, ranging from an eighth grade remedial course for those reading at fourth level, up to a twelfth grade course on "A Depth Study of Shakespeare." In mathematics, courses range from those for students with a very low level of achievement up to courses in probabilities and in creative mathematics for the advanced math student. No attempt is made to schedule 50 English courses, 45 mathematics courses and 60 social studies courses in any single semester. But a typical student of average performance may expect to follow a tailor-made curriculum in his five years of high school.

Gillis stresses that the four quarter program was conceived also as a contribution to solving the problem of juvenile delinquency in Atlanta.

In Atlanta proper, according to John W. Letson, superintendent of schools, one third of the 36,000 high school students are now attending voluntary summer quarter sessions. This summer quarter has added $2 million to Atlanta's $85 million school budget.[9]

In the total Atlanta metropolitan area, including Fulton County, the schools release 150,000 teenagers to roam the streets at the beginning of June, according to Gillis. The kids cannot find employment. Many of them have nothing to do but stand on the street corner and look for excitement. "With this program properly implemented, so that these kids can be guided into meaningful summer educational experience without having to pay tuition, we will have moved a long way towards solving the problem of the long hot summer," Gillis concludes. In practice, however, the Fulton County program has worked out primarily as a longer-than-usual summer school on an optional basis. The State has not been able to appropriate sufficient funds to permit exercise of the attendance option in other quarters. With enthusiasm for the system's early experience, Gillis states, "This program has the potential of changing the face of education, not only in Georgia, but on the national level. The authors might add one comment on Fulton County's pioneering work. The failure to implement the attendance plan in the fall, winter and spring quarters demonstrates once again that voters are reluctant to appropriate extra school funds for enrichment, or for "more learning." The public's interest lies primarily in economy!

MICHIGAN'S DEPTH STUDY

The Michigan State Board of Education has also undertaken a broad feasibility study of the possibilities for improving education, and effecting operating and capital economies through some form of year round school. The $100,000 study is being carried out in eight key school districts about the state.[10] a major stone in the state's study of year-round education is "The Four-Quarter Staggered School Year, A Feasibility Study to Extend the School Year," which was published by the Utica Community School District, Utica, Michigan, in July, 1970. The Utica Community Schools are located in the east central portion of Macomb county, due north of Detroit, and due east of Pontiac. The 65-mile-square district now has a few more than 20,000 pupils, twice the number it had in 1960. This number is expected to double in the next ten years.

The primary conclusion of the exhaustive 580-page feasibility study is that the implementation of a mandatory four-quarter school plan will save nearly $100 million in construction costs for the district during the years 1971 through 1980. This figure is based on 1970 dollars, according to Phillip Runkel, superintendent of Utica

schools, and the figure might easily soar to $150 million, with infla-
tion in construction costs and continued high interest rates. In his
foreword, Runkel states, "I personally believe that this country is in
the midst of a general year-round educational movement. How fast,
how far, and to where it takes us, no one can predict."

As part of the feasibility study, the school district conducted an
area-wide study of public opinion on calendar revision. The mandatory four-quarter staggered plan "would alienate the vast majority
(88 percent) of the voters, who prefer to take their vacations in the
summer months." However, 66 percent of the parents polled indicated that they approve an optional approach to year-round education "as a means to improve the quality of educational opportunities
for their boys and girls, provided that there is "no extra cost to the
taxpayers."

Mr. Runkel reports that Utica educators are looking forward to a
new, "restructured" curriculum, changing the present two-semester
system to a quarter one, and providing shorter, more flexible class
units. The study has indicated that tax dollars will be saved in a
year-round school program through:

> Greater educational efficiency
> Reduced capital outlay
> Improved instructional salaries, based on year-round employ-
>   ment
> Reduced transportation costs
> Reduced building and maintenance costs.

The sponsors of the Utica studies, however, choose to dabble their
toes in the stream of year-round education. The administration
would devote two years to the feasibility study (which is now complete), and then spend three years in "the communications phase,"
offering the community an opportunity to learn more about the
plan. Midway through the seventies, the Utica administration proposes a "tooling up" phase, which would be devoted to preparing
curriculum and other facets for a pilot program. The years from
1974 to 1979 would be devoted to a five-year pilot, experimental
program, in a limited number of the twelve schools in the district.
Finally, in 1980, the school board would be asked to implement
year-round schools in Utica. No such leisurely pace was possible in
the crowded Valley View district in Will County, Illinois. The authors hasten to add, however, that Runkel and his associates have

performed a monumental service in researching and setting forth the history of the year-round school movement, and in identifying and describing the broad variety of specific programs that fall under the broad umbrella of "year-round education."

CLARION'S CONTROLLED TEST

Credit belongs also to John D. McLain, of the Research-Learning Center, Clarion State College, Clarion, Pennsylvania, for advancing the rationale of year-round education, as well as setting forth some interesting specific proposals for total reform of the present day school. As this book is being written, McLain is developing a "research-demonstration model" of the "Flexible All-Year School" as a learning system component of the research-learning center. In this program, he intends to carry out exploratory programs on life-span education from nursery school through the secondary levels, with a study group of approximately 300 students.

Even more interesting than Mr. McLain's broad-ranging program of research in all educational aspects of the year-round school is his advancement of a philosophy embracing the sociological implications.[11] One of his main reasons for instituting year-round classes is his desire to schedule vacations for pupils, teachers and parents at any period during the calendar year. The educator would reform the existing contracts between management and labor, which generally specify summer vacations, to make possible rotation of all worker vacations throughout the calendar year. The habit of summer vacations, he holds, arose from two considerations: workers wanted to take their time off when the children were out of school; management wanted to schedule vacations in the summer, when school teachers were available to add to the temporary labor force.

Working against the existing pattern, McLain holds, is the increasing demand for skilled, rather than unskilled labor. This makes it difficult for plants to use temporary vacation help, and reduces the opportunities for both teachers and high school students in the summer work force. Also a factor is the constantly increasing cost of fringe benefits, which accrue to the temporary worker, as well as to the skilled, permanent employe. Under a year-round, rotating vacation policy, these benefits would cost employers less, and they would all accrue to permanent staff members. McLain also reasons that a scheme of rotating vacations for the full year in industry would create one, new, permanent job for every eleven workers employed at present. This would help reduce national unemployment, he holds. On a national basis, this would create more than a million jobs. Needless to say, it would also decrease the presently rising unemployment of teachers during summer months. McLain points to a recent change in the basic contract of the United Steelworkers union, which not only permits vacations at any time of the year, but pays a $30 weekly premium to the worker who takes his vacation during "off seasons."

In urging adoption of "The Flexible All-Year School," McLain takes a penetrating look at all aspects of education, and considers the change in calendar as only one aspect of an overall reform movement. His first concern is with the "knowledge explosion." No longer, he holds, can formal education consist of storing in a child's mind, through memorization, all of the facts that educators once believed to make up the needed body of knowledge. Rather, the current teaching technique is to teach children to learn solutions and how to solve problems, to help children develop the process of finding out the knowledge they will need at any point in time through understanding and utilization of retrieval systems. He summarizes "that children need to learn how to find information, how to think, how to analyze situations, and how to make decisions."

McLain also sees the all-year school as a potential solution to the high school "dropout" problem and the other problems of the educationally, culturally, and economically disadvantaged. "A dropout is usually a child who has failed one or more years of school, and is failing to keep up with his group," McLain reasons. "He drops out when he leaves school in conflict with authority (whether home, school, or law) and has no chance to come back and make up the time he has lost, or when he establishes out-of-school relationships during the long summer vacation and prefers not to return to school." McLain suggests that in the Flexible All-Year School, the student could not "fail" a year of school; he could resume his learning where he left off, so he could return to school any time and would not need to be out on the streets during a long summer vacation. He adds that the child of the migrant worker could also enter and leave school with less loss of continuity in education.

Interestingly, McLain's approach to acceleration differs sharply than that of the New York solons. "The gifted child," he writes, "may pursue any significant aspect of learning as fully as he can, and progress as rapidly as he is able. . . . This does not mean that the rate or progression will be accelerated so that students will graduate in fewer than the traditional twelve years. This could be done if there is reason for it, but, in general, there is no need to get youth onto the labor market earlier. In fact, the reverse is true. Children should, therefore, be encouraged to pursue knowledge in depth in individualized, ever-branching programs, rather than following a narrow, linear path to early completion with minimum standards."

INDIVIDUAL LEARNING GOAL

McLain emphasizes that the continuous, year-round school fosters individualized instruction and that it adapts well to either repetition of a portion of the year's work or to the taking of enrichment subjects, without the stigma of "failing to pass" a year in school. He contends that the year-round school will include most of the major, current innovations in education which are designed to give flexibility, as well as depth and breadth to learning experience. "The variability in group sizes, both in terms of learning situations and fluctuation in enrollment due to changing vacation schedules, makes team teaching a natural approach to staff utilization," McLain continues. ". . .Such a school is automatically 'non-graded' even though 'multiage grouping' may or may not be used, depending upon the situation.

"To maximize the learning environment, multimedia and laboratory approaches will be used. Computer assisted instruction, microteaching and other techniques will be used to help provide an enriched environment that will provide each learner challenging experiences appropriate to him in terms of his perception, abilities, maturity level, rate of maturation, societal demands and objectives."

McLain concludes that the all-year school will break the "lock step" in education, and will facilitate an educational system really designed to educate all children and youth.

McLain has contributed to the national promotion of the year-round school by convening a "Second National Seminar on Year-Round Education," held in April, 1970, in Harrisburg, Pennsylvania. Similar seminars have been held in the last two years in Fayetteville, Arkansas; DeKalb, Illinois; Champaign, Illinois; and Cocoa Beach, Florida. These seminars have enabled many educators to exchange ideas, and to contribute creative thinking to the problems (and there are many) of calendar revision.

National interest in year-round education has been promoted extensively by the industry-oriented National School Calendar Study Committee, Minneapolis. George M. Jensen, founder, served as president of the Minneapolis Board of Education for several years and worked aggressively, but unsuccessfully, to promote year-round utilization of the city's school buildings. He has also employed prolific public relations counsel, who has been successful in "planting" articles on the economics of year-round school plans in a number of major periodicals, including *Reader's Digest, Saturday Review,* and *Better Homes & Gardens.*

Another prolific and highly effective promoter of the year-round school concept is Robert M. Beckwith, manager, Educational Department, Illinois State Chamber of Commerce, Chicago. Beckwith has waged a continuous campaign on legislative, industry and school board fronts, and deserves much credit for bringing a number of Illinois schools to the brink of calendar revision.[12]

BEDROOM SUBURB STEPS OUT

A single public school in one midwestern school district in 1969 adopted a revised school calendar that is strikingly similar to that developed by the Valley View District in the fall of 1968 and implemented in the summer of 1970. This is the Becky-David School in the Francis Howell School district, located along the Missouri River, to the west of St. Charles, Missouri, which is a large suburb of St. Louis.[13] Like the Valley View District, the Francis Howell District is in the process of rapid change from a primarily rural population to an exurban population. It has been called "the bedroom of St. Louis."

Implementation of a year-round school program here, as in Valley View, was stimulated by the shortage of available classroom seats and by the shortage of available bonding power for new construction (although Missouri permits its school districts to bond to ten percent of assessed valuation, compared to five percent in Illinois). In the 1969-70 school year, the Francis Howell District had an enrollment of 3,471 elementary students (1 through 8) and 683 secondary students (9 through 12), for a total enrollment of 4,154. Some 992 students are housed in the Francis Howell Junior High School. The rated capacity of the entire system is 3,430 students, compared with the 4,154 enrollment. Approximately 1,546 students were enrolled in the Becky-David Elementary School, serving grades 1-6, which had a rated capacity of 1,300 students in 45 rooms.

The Francis Howell administration developed what it calls a nine-week, three-week plan, which like the Valley View plan, calls for distributing the normal three-month summer vacation through a series of four three-week vacations during the remainder of the school year. This continuous school year plan was scheduled only in the double-size Becky-David School, because this was the only building large enough to accommodate four classrooms for each grade in the school. The attendance area was divided geographically into four groups, northeast, southeast, southwest, and northwest. As at Valley View, three groups or "tracks" are in attendance through most of the school year, while one group is on vacation. Unlike Valley View's 45-15 Continuous School Year Plan, the number of school days assigned to each group is not exactly equal. The school district has attempted to start classes and vacations on Mondays, and to end them on Fridays. To make this possible, different quarters range from 42 to 46 school days, and some quarters are divided into 32-, 11-, 18-, and 10-day segments.

The school board has conducted a continuing public relations and information program, accompanied by an opinion research effort. In general, replies from parents have indicated that approximately 42 percent support the program, while 24 percent oppose it. Sixty percent of the voters indicated that they would support a bond issue to finance air conditioning of the Becky-David School. The Danforth Foundation of St. Louis has made a grant to conduct an educational evaluation of the Francis Howell District, comparing the performance of the students at the Becky-David School with that of the students at three other elementary schools in the district.

We believe that at the present time Francis Howell, Atlanta, and Valley View are the only school systems in the country conducting year-round programs. In the Francis Howell district, the continuous school year plan is followed in only one school.* The Atlanta program is basically a voluntary summer school plan, since at present funds do not permit students to take winter quarters off. Only at Valley View is an entire school system operated currently on a staggered group plan, giving every student an equal time in school throughout the year, with vacations in each quarter.

In closing this review of the status of the year-round school in

*In April 1971, the Francis Howell Board of Education voted to extend the nine-three plan to all schools.

various systems around the country, the authors note that the widespread publicity given the Valley View schools has resulted in intensive interest in the 45-15 plan among other school districts in Illinois. Two other Chicago suburban school districts are actively studying the 45-15 plan at this time in hope of placing it into effect in 1972 or 1973. Also James F. Redmond, Chicago's superintendent of schools, has asked his Board of Education to authorize a pilot year-round school program in several high schools. The Chicago program —which has been proposed off and on since 1955—will probably get under way in the 1972-73 school year.

6

Test Tube

It was almost inevitable that Valley View School District 96 of Will County, Illinois, would be the site of a major breakthrough in year-round education. For in this semiurban district are compounded most of the problems that have beset soaring suburban districts since the end of World War II.

The Valley View District lies on high, but gently rolling, rich farm land in the northwestern corner of Will County in Illinois. The 40-mile square area of the district is bisected diagonally by Interstate Highway I-55, the main traffic artery between Chicago and St. Louis, Missouri. I-55 replaces the long crumbling US-66, the Santa Fe Trail made famous in John Steinbeck's *Grapes of Wrath*. Downtown Chicago lies 30 miles or 45 minutes to the northeast via I-55, known as Adlai Stevenson Expressway within the city. The historic town of Joliet, named for Father Louis Joliet, the French Jesuit explorer, lies ten miles to the south of the heart of the district. The district gets its name, Valley View, from the fact that it is located on high ground overlooking the Des Plaines River, and the Chicago Sanitary and Ship Canal, main arteries in the Great Lakes to the Gulf Waterway, one of the world's busiest channels.

The Des Plaines river gives the Valley View District one of its few industries, the large limestone quarries of the General Dynamics Corporation, which furnished much of the crushed stone for building the southwestern railroads and the highways of Illinois. The river also supplies Illinois soft coal and cooling water for a huge steam power generating plant of the Commonwealth Edison Company, which accounts for approximately 32 percent of the $127 million estimated

1970-71 assessed valuation of the Valley View District. The district is laced with high-tension lines carrying power to Chicago and Northeastern Illinois. Just outside the district, and contributing nothing to its tax revenues, are the large Argonne National Laboratory, operated by the University of Chicago for the U.S. Atomic Energy Commission; a large oil refinery, which receives its crude petroleum in barges along the Illinois-Mississippi Waterway; and the immense Statesville Penitentiary, built as a model prison in the early twenties to augment the famous Joliet Penitentiary. Many of the present residents of the Valley View District work in these facilities lying outside of the District. Others work in large tractor and farm equipment plants in the southwestern suburbs of Chicago and in Joliet, which is also a center for producing steel wire and fencing. About ten percent of the workers living in the district are employed by the many interstate and regional trucking firms whose depots are located strategically south and west of the City of Chicago.

The Valley View District contains no major shopping centers. There are small neighborhood food marts in both Romeoville and Bolingbrook, the two incorporated communities within the district. Residents turn to Joliet, or to Oakbrook shopping centers, approximately fifteen miles away, for their principal purchases. Accordingly, there is almost no sales tax revenue to support municipal functions within the district.

FROM 89 TO 6,950

Valley View Elementary School District 96 was formed in the summer of 1953 by combining four one-room country schools into a single consolidated District. The total number of students registered in the first year was 89, which compares with more than 6,950 during the current 1970-71 school year. There were five teachers; two are still employed by the district—Miss Eileen Ward as a junior high school English teacher, and Kenneth L. Hermansen, co-author of this book, then and now as superintendent of schools. The 1970-71 staff of District 96 totals 275. The agrarian school trustees who organized District 96 gladly gave up their seats on the combined board to make possible the initiation of a general science program at the seventh and eighth grade levels. They were concerned primarily with upgrading the educational offerings for their children—a concern that is still uppermost in the minds of the heterogeneous board, on which the few remaining farmers of the district are still represented.

District 96 coasted comfortably, in so far as expansion was concerned, until the fall of 1959. The official average daily attendance for the 1958-59 school year was 219. The district's assessed valuation had grown to $55 million, thanks to construction at the Commonwealth Edison power plant, and there was a comfortable $254,359 assessed property valuation to support *each* student. But, then came the avalanche. Elementary school population jumped 260 percent to 542 as the first immigrants from Chicago began to fill up the Hampton Park prefabricated housing project, developed by Alexander Construction company, largest dealer for the nation's largest manufacturer of preassembled, panelized houses, National Homes Corporation of Lafayette, Indiana. The village of Romeoville, headquarters of the school district, had enjoyed a comfortable, rural population of 400 in the 1950 Census. With the impact of Alexanders' rows of prefabricated houses, the village was destined to grow to 3,574 in the 1960 Census; 6,358 in a special census taken in the mid-sixties; and to nearly 9,000 in the 1970 Census. Lagging only slightly behind was the new village of Bolingbrook, at the intersection of I-55 with Illinois 53, which had jumped to a population of 5,357 in a special census in the mid-sixties, and a population of nearly 8,000 in the 1970 Census.

School population soared accordingly; the Valley View District served an elementary school population of 900 in 1960-61; 3,318 in 1965-66, and 6,603 in September, 1970, when the 45-15 Continuous School Plan was in force.

The financial plight of the district was compounded continually. Thanks to the arrival of the Commonwealth Edison plant on the taxrolls, the assessed valuation per pupil had reached a peak of $261,475 in 1957-58, the year before Alexander Construction Company's project began to flood the district with school-age children. By 1966-67, the assessed value per pupil had dropped to $25,926, and by the fall of 1970, the 1969 taxes collected were on an assessed valuation of $17,553 per pupil, just one fifteenth of the peak valuation in 1957-58. In Illinois, schools are supported approximately two thirds from taxes on real and personal property, and one third from State aid. The school population of District 96 was affected by another fact. Approximately two-thirds of the residents of the District are Roman Catholics—largely of Italian, Polish and Irish descent—

workers who have moved from their homes on the west, southwest, and south sides of Chicago when the black population increased there. Only a fraction of the children from these families attend Catholic parochial elementary schools—approximately 400. And the Joliet Catholic Diocese has no plans for increasing its school facilities in the area.

TRACT BUILDERS RUN WILD

Home building has lagged during the past two years in the district, due to the high cost of construction and the high interest rates. This has had the temporary effect of sending the district approximately 10 percent fewer students than had been estimated in school administration projections for the 1970-71 school year. However, the end is nowhere near in sight. Alexander Construction Company still sells at the "bottom" of the price scale, and has plenty of land to continue its pace of operations for at least ten years more. In addition, three of the largest nationwide real estate developers operating in the booming Chicago market have begun active promotion of new home construction covering the entire current price spectrum—from approximately $15,000 (including land and landscaping) to $40,000. These home builders are Hoffman-Rosner Corporation, which has built the large northwestern suburbs of Schaumburg and Hoffman Estates; Centex-Winston Corporation, builder of the large Elk Grove Village residential and industrial complex; and Kaufman & Broad, largest developer in the Chicago area, with homes under way in a dozen subdivisions encircling the city.

William A. Levitt & Son, nationally-publicized developers of Levittown, Long Island, and Levittown, Pennsylvania, has also acquired substantial acreage in District 96 for investment and "future development." Each of the "big builders" is currently advertising attractively priced homes and condominiums (deeded out multiple family units) in weekly full-page advertisements in the Chicago metropolitan daily newspapers. Conservative estimates given District 96 by the five large developers operating in the area indicate a total pace of well over 1,000 new homes a year. With the land that the developers now own, fully developed, it is reasonable to expect that Valley View Elementary School District 96 will have to provide kindergarten and eight years of "grammar school" education for 20,000 children by the time the next (1980) decennial Census comes around.

Although the majority of the voters and taxpayers in District 96 are blue collar workers (truckers and factory employees), they have historically supported the District to the greatest possible degree, voting almost continual increases in the educational tax rate, and in bond issues to build new schools.

When the school district was organized, in 1953, the total school tax rate (excluding bonds and interest) was 42.4 cents per $100 of assessed valuation. In that year the district's voters passed their first building bond referendum, projecting the eight-room Valley View School, on Naperville Road, to the northwest of Romeoville. The district had approximately 500 homes, and 143 students.

In 1959, the year that the school enrollment doubled in only one year, a 23-room addition to the Valley View School was approved by the voters and constructed. In 1961, when the enrollment was approaching 1,200, the voters approved a tax rate of 87.5 cents per $100 of assessed valuation. The Park View School in Romeoville, the present administrative headquarters of the district, was erected in 1962. The tax rate was increased to 97.2 cents. In 1963, when the enrollment jumped to 2,424 students, the tax rate was increased again to $1.224. In the following year, the district built an air-conditioned addition to Park View School, and constructed the new 30-room North View School. The tax rate jumped to $1.8450. In the following year the voters boosted the tax rate to $2.068, and the contemporary West View Junior High School was completed and occupied. Again, in 1967, as the enrollment increased to 4,325 students, the tax rate was increased to $2.3940, inching up to $2.40 (in all accounts except bond and interest) in 1968, when enrollment reached 4,942 students. In this year, the school board directed the administration "to design a sound educational program for the extended use of school facilities and personnel." The pace of construction continued: The Brookview School was completed and occupied in February, 1969, and the Ridge View School was completed and occupied in December, 1969.

VOTERS BACK REFERENDUMS

Historically, according to James Bingle, president of the District 96 Board of Education, and local tax assessor, the voters have approved almost every increase requested in the educational, building or transportation tax rates, or in the bonds and interest rate to finance new construction. The voters continued their historic support of the schools at a referendum, August 15, 1970, at which they approved a higher educational tax rate and $2.6 million in bond issues, under the five percent of assessed valuation allowed by Illinois law. The total school tax rate moved up to $2.674.

Bingle estimates that the average home in the district is assessed at $9,000. A homeowner in the northern part of Hampton Park, near Park View School, pays a total tax bill of approximately $520, based on a combined rate of $5.719 for all school, city, county, sanitary, forest preserve and mosquito abatement levies. A typical Bolingbrook home owner, also assessed at $9,000, pays approximately $508 during 1971 on his 1970 taxes. Of this amount, approximately $240 is paid into the total budget of School District 96.

It is interesting to note, and significant to the story of Valley View schools, that relations have always been excellent between the school district and the Commonwealth Edison Company, the largest taxpayer. The public utility has protested its taxes in only one year—when its levies were jumped high enough to warrant appealing the assessment—an appeal which the company won.

Because of Commonwealth Edison's status as a major taxpayer, the School Board has always given its marketing and sales representatives a full hearing. Late in the fifties, when expansion began to hit Valley View with full force, Edison representatives prepared a comprehensive analysis of the relative cost of heating the schools by electricity, gas, and oil, as well as the costs of providing optional air-conditioning. The utility's analysis took into account all capital costs, such as chimneys, boiler rooms, hot water piping, electric transformer vaults, and over-sized wiring that would ultimately accommodate air-conditioning. The case for electric heat was convincing, and beginning with the Park View School's first 24 classroom section, in 1962, electric heat was installed in all buildings, and all buildings were wired to accommodate ultimate installation of refrigeration to give complete, year-round air conditioning to the system. Thanks to the aggressive marketing of the electric company, and the foresight of earlier school board members, summer cooling was included in the provisions for all school buildings erected after 1962, when the first Park View section was built. Thus, when the school board made its ultimate decision to go to a year-round program, the only building that needed to be air-conditioned was the central portion of the Park View School. This air conditioning was installed during the

1970-71 school year at a cost of approximately $80,000, ready for the second summer season under the 45-15 Continuous School Year Plan. Fortunately, there was a sufficient surplus of classrooms during July and August, 1970, to accommodate most of the summer school students in classrooms equipped with air-conditioning.

KINDERGARTEN "BREAKS BACK"

Despite Valley View's record for going "all out" to vote operating and construction funds for its schools, the "straw that broke the camel's back" came in the spring of 1968. The Illinois Legislature, in the closing days of the 66th General Assembly, voted to make kindergarten compulsory in all public school districts in the State. Because of its constant race to keep school capacity apace with enrollments, District 96 had never offered kindergarten, although the pre-school class is common in most schools in the Chicago metropolitan area and in the City of Chicago. The fall kindergarten enrollment expected for 1970 was estimated at 1,320. This immediately increased the number of pupil stations required in the school system by 660, allowing for double kindergarten sessions. Thus the school, in a single year, would need to provide approximately 20 kindergartens, in addition to caring for the rapid, continuous expansion in all eight elementary grades, which are averaging 600 new students a year.

Despite the fact that two new elementary buildings were scheduled to open during 1970, there was no foreseeable way of providing the 20 kindergartens needed. With the Legislature's edict of 1968, the Valley View schools were faced with drastic and momentous decisions.

7

45-15 In Valley View

Late in 1967, James Bingle, then a member of District 96's Board of Education, dropped a brown envelope on the desk of Ken Hermansen, superintendent of schools. The packet was from the National School Calendar Study Association, Minneapolis, Minnesota. A parent had given Bingle the packet from the Twin City group. The envelope contained half a dozen magazine reprints of articles from *Reader's Digest, Parents, Saturday Review,* and other general magazines, and an article from *School Management* suggesting a dozen or more, year-round school calendars. Most of them, incidentally were based on the nine-month, three-month staggered quarter system, a plan that would have turned one fourth of the school system's children out of school in midwinter. Even though the "nine-three" calendar proposal was patently unsuitable to parents in a northern climate, the superintendent studied all of the proposals, in the hope that the year-round school might offer a solution to the Valley View housing dilemma.

Without arriving at a satisfactory solution to his problem, Hermansen went one step further in March, 1968. Addressing the Valley View faculty workshop on "School Trends in the Seventies," the superintendent predicted a number of changes—team teaching, the ungraded school, and the then seemingly remote possibility that school children and teachers might attend classes the year round. There were a few questions, a few comments pro and con, but there was not much serious interest in the proposal to revise the school calendar. However, the subject did not lie dormant.

Hermansen began to sketch out various proposals on bits of paper; none of the publicized plans seemed practical for elementary school.

However, the superintendent felt that there was some merit to the nine-month, three-month staggered quarter system in high school (Lockport West High School, which serves the Valley View area, is governed by a separate Board of Education). Possibly the year-round idea could be extended to the West View Junior High School. But this possibility was dismissed because it would force different vacation patterns within families with students in the primary and intermediate grades, and because the number of students affected was not great enough to have any impact on the total district problem. Hermansen toyed with splitting the long, three-month vacation into four, short three-week vacations, but for the time being abandoned the idea. His "scratch pad" calendar couldn't fit in all of the holidays, "institute" days and "snow" days, and still fulfill Illinois statutory requirements that children receive at least 180 full days of instruction.

In June, 1968, Hermansen called Jim Gove (then staff director of multimedia and research) and asked him to gather everything that had been published on year-round schools. If necessary, the superintendent said, contact the administrators in those school districts that have adopted year-round programs. As the mass of available literature (enough to fill a file drawer) filtered in, Gove found little real help.

SOURCES MOSTLY VERBIAGE

"I found out that there was a lot of educational verbiage," Gove said. "But when you read it over, you find out that there are just ideas and theories advanced by various laymen and educators. The school calendar revisionists were mainly 'talkers,' and not 'doers,' and they had been talking the subject for years—ever since the days of Bluffton and Newark and Aliquippa."

The literature did produce some useful information, however. It became clear to the Valley View administrators that there is a vast difference between mandatory programs (such as those instituted at Aliquippa and Ambridge) and "voluntary" summer school programs, such as those of Newark and Nashville in the twenties, and Atlanta, Georgia in the sixties. Obviously, a voluntary program could not make a dent in a critical classroom shortage; this had been proved wherever the student and his parents were permitted an option. If a year-round plan was to increase the number of available classrooms and school seats throughout the school year, it would have to be mandatory.

Teachers continued to discuss the year-round school; they were apparently intrigued by Hermansen's March presentation. It was a common topic in the teachers' lounges and the cafeterias, especially among the male teachers in the junior high school and the intermediate grades, who sensed an opportunity to increase their total annual income without working at jobs for which they were not well prepared during the summer months. Ultimately, their talk filtered out into the community, and, of course, ultimately to members of the Board of Education.

Suddenly, during the last Board of Education meeting in July, 1968, Harold Lindstrom, who was then vice president of the Board, asked, "What are you doing about year-round schools?

The administration replied, "We are investigating it. It is going to take a lot of work. There is no possible way of adopting any kind of a year-round school plan until the 1971-72 school year."

The Board members, especially Bingle and Lindstrom, were adamant. They said, "We want some reports, and we want to get moving!" The administration agreed to report in two weeks.

At the mid-August meeting, the administrators reported that the vast majority of so-called "authorities" on year-round education favored the nine-month, three-month staggered quarter plan, which had failed at Aliquippa and Ambridge, Pennsylvania, in the thirties. Although the Board members agreed that this four-quarter staggered year plan would prove unpopular with the community, they were insistent that there must be some other calendar combination that could achieve the same goals without all of the objections. Compulsory kindergarten was only two years away, they argued, and the Board simply did not have the bonding power to provide the 20 additional kindergarten rooms that would be needed in September, 1970.

A DETERMINED BOARD

Sensing the Board's determination, the administration had prepared a formal resolution. It read, "I move that the Board of Education, School District 96 of Will County, hereby directs the administrative team to begin forthright the investigative procedures for updating the school calendar, utilizing more calendar days of the year, staff, and equipment, and giving periodic reports to the Board of Education. The new calendar designed shall be recommended to the school board, and instituted on or before the 1971-72 school year." Harold Lindstrom made the motion; Jim Bingle seconded; the vote was unanimous. The board also approved a referendum, to be held in September, 1968, to approve a bond issue, to build two small schools, Ridgeview and Brookview. This bond issue, approved by the voters in September, exhausted, for the time being, District 96's bonding power for future construction. The heat was on. The action was decisive. The administration went to work.

Jim Gove found that his duties as director of research and multi-media did not permit him enough time to give the new year-round school assignment the attention it required. Therefore, the administration, in early September, 1968, secured Board approval to assign Pat Page, a typing teacher, to be released half-time to help Gove with development of the "Valley View Year-Round School Plan."

Page was instructed to research the feasibility, and the pros and cons, of various staggered group proposals. After two weeks time he came up with a "nine-three plan." It was the familiar four-quarter, staggered group plan, already judged impractical by the administration, because of potential Community resistance to a compulsory, three-month vacation for one fourth of the students in midwinter.

Hermansen and Gove then directed Page to work out a nine-week, three-week program, which would give every student four three-week vacations a year. Page spent another two weeks on the plan, and then confirmed what Hermansen had already determined—that it was impossible to start school on a Monday; end school on a Friday; get in all of the institute, holiday and snow days; and still have enough days left over to fulfill the state requirement of 180 days of instruction.

This problem concerned both Hermansen and Gove greatly, because they did not want to discriminate, in any way, against any group of students. One of the mandatory goals, the administrators felt, was to provide each group of children with exactly the same number of days of vacation, of holidays, and of instruction.

Gove then told Page, "One of the things we are going to have to do, is to try to forget as much as possible of all the traditional thinking that we have been exposed to in our educational course teachings in college, and in our experience. Let's throw out every sacred cow to start with. Why don't you list every school day—every Monday through every Friday—on a sheet of paper, and number them from one through two hundred sixty one (leaving out all Saturdays and Sundays and holidays)? Forget about fiscal years. Start the students anytime, and finish up their school years anytime. But try to get 180 days in for compulsory school attendance!" The goal was still to find a nine-week, three-week solution.

CALENDAR BACKS UP

Around October 1, Page came in with what the administrators called their road map. Since the compulsory 180 days of instruction could be divided into four quarters of 45 days each, and the desired three weeks of vacation would take 15 class days, Page dubbed the plan "The 45-15 Continuous School Year Plan." Page had arrived at his "school solution" by working backwards from Monday, August 16, 1971—which was exactly three weeks before the last eighth grade graduate would begin classes in Lockport West High School. The first student, it was discovered, would have to enter school Tuesday, June 30, 1970—one day before the beginning of the 1970-71 school fiscal year. But the important thing—"the breakthrough in year-round education"—had been achieved. Here was a workable school calendar that would give every child, and every family, the same number of days of instruction, vacations and holidays. Every family would enjoy not only a summer vacation from school, but one in the fall, one in the winter, and one in the spring. Just to make sure there were no pitfalls, Page went back to his scratchpads, and worked out "45-15" calendars for the next five school years. Even with the federal and state provisions for ten Monday holidays a year, the plan was workable for at least five years ahead. It was therefore submitted to the Board of Education at an October meeting, and adopted officially.

The reader can understand the 45-15 plan best by referring to the four-color calendar that Page prepared for submission to the parents in the district, and to the board. Because he was working in the multimedia department, which is concerned with audio-visual presentation, Page's demonstration calendar was worked out on a series of illustration board sheets, taped together at the edges so that they made a continuous display 34 feet long. (See fig. 1. Also see foldout calendar opposite page 84.)

FIGURE 1. J. Patrick Page, Valley View Schools' director of research, developed this 34-foot long 45-15 calendar to demonstrate the workings of the year-round school to parent groups and to State Superintendent of Public Instruction officials.

The 45-15 Continuous School Plan—as evolved at Valley View Schools—is really quite simple.

Essentially, the entire September, 1970, student body of 6,514 was divided into four groups or "tracks," each including approximately 1,625 students. To simplify the arithmetic, let us assume that the total school population is 6,400, and that there are 1,600 students in each track.

On the first day that the plan is placed in effect, one fourth of the students, making up group or track "A," begin nine weeks, or 45 school days of classes. The number actually attending classes is 1,600, the entire population of Group "A."

On the sixteenth day of classes, another 1,600 students, this time Group "B" enters school, bringing the total attendance up to 3,200 students, Group "A" remains in school.

On the 31st day of classes, the third group, Track "C" enters school, bringing the total attendance in the school up to 4,800 students, the system's theoretical capacity. Every classroom and every seat is filled.

On the 46th school day that the plan is in effect, Group "A" has completed its first cycle or quarter of 45 days, and goes on vacation. The seats occupied during the previous 45 days by the members of Group "A" are taken by the 1,600 students of Group "D," who have not yet entered school. The school buildings are still filled to capacity, 4,800 students, but one fourth of all of the students are on vacation, this time Group "A."

From the 46th day on, the schedule keeps repeating itself, much like the old musical round, "Row, Row, Row Your Boat," in which one fourth of the chorus is always singing the opening lines.

Thus, each student in the school, from kindergarten through eighth grade, attends classes for 45 days, and then enjoys vacation for 15 days. This rhythm is repeated four times a year, so that each student attends school for the legal minimum of 180 (4 times 45) days, and spends 60 days on vacation in four segments spaced around the year—one in summer, one in the fall, one in winter, and one in the spring.

In addition, all students enjoy an additional week of vacation at Christmas, one at Easter, and one at July 1. During these standard, traditional vacations, the school custodians do their major maintenance and cleaning work within the classrooms.

MORE KIDS, FEWER DOLLARS

The reader may ask, "Why all of this rotation; this game of musical chairs?" The answer is that the school system's buildings total capacity is increased by one third (in our model instance, from 4,800 students to 6,400 students) making possible very substantial savings in construction costs, bond amortization and interest payments.

The 45-15 Continuous School Plan is strictly a device for providing schooling for more children at less cost. It is purely a revision of the school calendar, designed to give all families in the school district an equal opportunity for education and for vacation. The total number of school days remains the same (180 days in Illinois and most other states). The plan is not intended primarily to increase the amount of learning, to provide makeup time for students who fall behind in one or more subjects, or to provide "enrichment." It is not meant as a plan for "baby sitting," or for keeping teenagers off the streets in summer time, although this would be a bonus advantage to a high school district.

IMPACT ON EDUCATION

The reader will find, however, as he proceeds to the chapters on "Teachers" and "Children," that the introduction of the 45-15 Continuous School Plan has had far-reaching impact on the education of the children, and on the stability and quality of the faculty. The cost of education has not increased—in fact a projection of estimated costs for the 1970-71 school year indicates a two to five percent reduction in the total cost of educating each child. This saving, which amounts to approximately $33 per student per year, was not planned for. It is simply one of the many bonus effects of the plan.

More than half of the women teachers, particularly those in the primary grades, have elected to teach for a traditional school year of 184 days, including the four "institute" days required by Illinois law. Of the men teachers, approximately 43 percent have elected to work for the maximum permitted under the plan, 274 days. Some of the 184-day teachers have elected to march "lock step" with their pupils —that is to stay with one group throughout the year, alternating 45 teaching days with 15 week days of vacation. Others have formed "co-operatives," a form of team-teaching, in which four teachers will split up the assignment of teaching four groups of children. Still others have elected to work for the traditional nine-month year, reserving summer (or another quarter) for advanced graduate work in education, or in their teaching specialty. Forgive the authors for their enthusiasm, but the fact is that the plan has offered "something for everybody" on the faculty, and accordingly has led to an easing of tensions that might have developed in teacher salary negotiations. It is significant that nearly half of the male teachers are earning from one third to one half more money annually from their primary job for which they were trained, teaching, instead of seeking summer employment in other areas.

Placing the plan in operation has presented problems, of course, for the administrators, who have had to tread on much uncharted ground. The major problem areas have been:

1. Working out legislation that will permit operation of the plan, and securing passage by the Illinois Legislature and approval of the Governor.

2. Working out the complexities of scheduling 6,500-plus students and some 260 teachers in six school buildings of different capacities four times a year. (This would have been impossible without the employment of the computer and its direction by a highly gifted educational systems analyst.)

3. Securing the approval and support of the community. (In this area it might be noted that only 20 of more than 3,000 families in District 96 asked to have their children's tracks changed.)

4. Negotiating a new contract, including a new salary "guide" with the teacher members of the Valley View Education Association.

5. Planning for, and initiating, an objective educational evaluation of the impact of 45-15 on the education of children in the district.

6. Planning for still more school buildings that will be designed with the special requirements of the 45-15 Continuous School Plan in mind.

At this point in time, after 45-15 has been in operation for nine months, the administrators can report that most of the problems, which loomed large at the time, have been solved easily through the co-operation of an unusually imaginative School Board and an understanding community. The remainder of this book is essentially a case history of the implementation of 45-15 in the Valley View schools, told largely in narrative form by the administrators and their staff members, as well as by other faculty members. The final chapters will look to the future, and offer some advice to other school boards and administrations, which may face the same fundamental problem of a shortage of space that dictated adoption of the continuous school plan at Valley View.

8

Community

Previous attempts to institute year-round education plans—particularly those at Newark and Aliquippa—have failed mainly for two reasons: administration and communications.

At Aliquippa it was resistance of parents, mainly to the four quarter staggered plan (which turned one fourth of the students out for three months in the winter) that led to the demise of the year-round school. Aliquippa's administrators were burdened, also, by the mass of personal contact and paperwork involved in rescheduling the entire school four times a year, a factor that has contributed to the strong resistance of most school administrators to the year-round school.

The initial success of 45-15 at Valley View is due primarily to intense, continuous concentration on communications (or public relations) with all of the elements of the community: parents, corporate taxpayers, faculty members, children, and state, federal and county educational departments.

As the authors mentioned at the close of the previous chapter, the successful operation of the 45-15 plan would have been impossible without reducing the administrative problem to manageable size. This was accomplished through skillful use of the electronic computer to accomplish the related tasks of scheduling children, teachers, classrooms and buses.

This chapter will be devoted largely to communications—with the members of the community; with the state, federal and county governments; with other school systems; and with the teachers. It will be told largely through the words of the staff members who conducted these activities, as recorded in cassette tape interviews conducted in the fall of 1970.

Essentially, the Valley View communications story is one of continuous efficient utilization of every channel of contact with those people whose approval was essential to the success of the plan. Although intensive use was made of the community and Chicago press, of radio and television, and audio-visual techniques, the key to the whole story is man-to-man contact.

Let it first be said that the superintendent of schools has traditionally enjoyed a relationship with parents that was both intimate and broad. He entered the Valley View District 96 in 1953, as both teacher and superintendent, when the school system operated five one-room schools for 89 students, and was required by Illinois law to employ a superintendent, because the total district population then barely exceeded 1,000.

CONTINUOUS BRINKSMANSHIP

The conduct of the superintendency has been an exercise in "brinksmanship" ever since.

The "dirt farmers" who merged four other districts into District 96 in 1953 were concerned because some of their schools were so small that they feared the Will County Superintendent of Schools would close them down and send their children to adjacent districts. Then, as ever since, the parents and board members were concerned with the quality of education. They wanted to replace the one-room schools with a central building, one that would provide facilities for science, physical education, and a cafeteria that would serve hot lunches. There were no buses; all students walked, or their parents drove them and picked them up.

During the 1953-54 school fiscal year, the voters approved a bond issue to construct the eight-room Valley View School, the first modern building in the area. There were no particular problems in passing the referendum. The district's 1953 assessed valuation was approximately $14.5 million, equal to approximately $162,000 for each of the 89 students enrolled. Communications were easy and simple. The superintendent and one of the seven School Board members called on virtually every family in the district. (Some meetings were doubled up at the homes of neighbors.) Thus, partly because the district was so small, the superintendent became personally acquainted with every parent, understood his attitudes, and knew which buttons to push to win favorable response.

NO ADVISORY COMMITTEE

There was not another bond referendum or a tax increase until 1959, when 23 rooms were added to the Valley View School to accommodate the rapidly soaring population of the National Homes Hampton Park subdivision in Romeoville. But the pattern of direct, person-to-person contact had proved successful; it was followed again and again, with success, and it has dominated the school system's public relations policies ever since. There was no need to follow what the military call "the school solution"—a citizens' advisory committee—because the Board and the administration were in direct, personal contact with the electorate. Altogether, over the past dozen years, the voters had approved seven bond issues, and an equal number of increases in the educational, building, and transportation tax rates.

The administration began "talking" about year-round school almost as soon as the first packet of literature from Jim Bingle was received. In April, 1968, the District's teachers asked the superintendent to give the principal talk at a teachers' workshop. He titled his talk, "Looking into the Seventies."

Already intrigued by the possibility that 96 might have to institute some kind of year-round program, Hermansen devoted most of his talk to the general subject of year-round education.

"The day will come in education, and sooner in District 96 than in most districts, when the year-round school will become a way of life," he predicted. The phrase, "way of life," became a favorite that has been echoed whenever an observer has referred to 45-15 as an "experiment."

Hermansen did not mention any particular plan—although most thinking then was centered on the four-quarter staggered enrollment scheme, and 45-15 had not yet been invented. Such a plan, he reasoned, would give the District one-third more utilization of its buildings. He also reasoned that teachers might find a solution to their long-stated demand for year-round pay.

YEAR-ROUND PAY FOR TEACHERS

"For a long time," Hermansen told the teachers, "You have been bemoaning the fact that you want year-round pay, and yet school boards and administrators have 'locked you out' for three months of the year. Year-round school," he continued, "would mean that a teacher who works a full year would receive additional pay (at the same daily rate) for the additional length of time spent in teaching.

"There would also be considerable flexibility in contracts. . . . A teacher could vacation in Florida or California in the winter, or take graduate work in any quarter of the year. . . . Student achievement could be increased."

The superintendent went on to project the impact of school calendar revision, in general terms, on parents, and their vacations, on employers, and on employment. At the end of his talk, the teachers were quite enthusiastic. They discussed the possibilities in their work rooms, lounges, and cafeterias. And they discussed the prospect at home, thus starting the grapevine going. Although no communications were directed to the community at large, the ball was rolling, and would soon arouse the "What goes on here?" query from the Board of Education.

Although Hermansen and Gove were getting nowhere in developing a specific plan suitable to Valley View (the three months winter vacation was considered an insurmountable obstacle) they kept the Board of Education informed of everything they found out through their mail and telephone inquiries around the country.

The first public intimation of the proposed calendar changes came in the August 1, 1968 issue of *The Beacon,* a weekly newspaper serving Bolingbrook and Romoeville. *The Beacon* reported that Harold Lindstrom, then vice president of the Board of Education, urged Hermansen to expedite plans for a twelve-month school, which the board had been discussing, and that he thought the target date should be 1970, when kindergarten would become compulsory in Illinois.

THREE YEARS CRAMMED INTO TWO

Hermansen and Gove both indicated that it would be almost impossible to implement a year-round program before 1971. The District, they said, would be largely exploring uncharted ground, since only one school in the country was making any progress in this direction. However, the board member was insistent. Gove therefore prepared a motion formally directing the "administration to make recommendations with the expressed purpose of up-dating the District 96 school calendar no later than the 1971-72 school year." This motion was introduced by Lindstrom, and was passed unanimously at the next board meeting. *The Beacon* commented, "What the above means is that the board wants a program on a 12-month school year." The "cat was out of the bag." Similar reports were carried within the next few weeks by the *Lockport Herald-News,* the *Hampton Park Herald* and the *Joliet Herald-News,* all of whom gave the plan major editorial support during the ensuing two years of implementation. The support of the local newspapers was facilitated by an "open book" press conference with the three editors concerned most directly with reporting District 96 affairs, which was held on September 10, 1968—at least three weeks before the 45-15 plan had been evolved.

On October 1, 1968, Hermansen made a 15-minute presentation of the over-crowded conditions in the district in a program conducted regularly by Boyd Bucher, Will County Superintendent of Schools, over radio station WJOL in Joliet. By this time, the District 96 thinking had arrived at a nine-week, three-week plan, which, Hermansen told the radio listeners, would overcome the primary objection of all four-quarter plans—giving unfair treatment to the fourth of the students who would be turned out of their classrooms for three months in midwinter. The "45-15 Continuous School Plan" was born within the next few days.

LEGISLATION NEEDED

On October 14, 1968, the Valley View administrators involved the State of Illinois; there were obviously several legal problems that had to be clarified. There was the need for new legislation—both on the school calendar and on such financial matters as the State aid formula and the calculation of payments into the Illinois Municipal Retirement Fund, to which all full-time Illinois teachers belong. Hermansen, Bucher, Gove, and Page called first on Wayne Newlon, Associate Superintendent of Public Instruction, the principal administrative assistant to Ray Page, who was then Illinois Superintendent of Public Instruction—an officer with broad authority over the public schools, as well as higher education institutions.

Newlon brought in Robert Grant, the OSPI specialist on organization; Everett Nicholas, assistant general counsel; and John Kirby, a staff member concerned primarily with the financial aspects of education—one of the principal concerns of the OSPI, which administers

State aid to education, as well as counseling the Legislature on its School Code. Pat Page had just completed his 34-foot-long visual presentation of the proposed 45-15 calendar for Valley View, and this was stretched out around the OSPI conference room.

Hermansen summarized District 96's problem, and was careful to state that he was coming to the State Superintendent for counsel and planning help, and not for additional State financial assistance. He said, "If this plan is going to succeed, financially, it will have to stand on its own feet." The superintendent reviewed all of the aspects of the plan which might require either changes in State legislation or administrative re-interpretation. Among his concerns were:

A redefinition of terms in the school calendar
Changing teacher relationships
Teachers' pensions
Illinois Municipal Retirement Fund
Social Security
School lunches
School transportation (busing)
Scheduling school calendars that might lap over into more than one school fiscal year.
State reimbursement. (It was suggested that this be increased by one-third, since only three fourths of the total membership of the school system would be in class on the days in which average daily attendance is calculated.)

Hermansen also asked for assistance from the OSPI in solving the problem of student scheduling; District 96 had neither computer equipment nor data processing experience. He stressed that the scheduling problem was important, because the District desired to include all of the children in one family in the same group or "track," and because both economy and the sheer problem of meeting time schedules necessitated scheduling all of the children from a neighborhood in the same track.

The State Superintendent's office quickly told the delegation that they had no expertise with scheduling, but recommended two sources—Statistical Tabulating Company, probably the largest independent computer service bureau in the country, which has a substantial clientele in high school and college scheduling, and the Educational Division of Compumatics, Inc., another computer service bureau, which was then headed by Dr. Benjamin Willis, former general superintendent of schools for the Chicago Board of Education, and the highest paid school administrator in the country. Both of these services were given consideration at a later date. The various staff members of the OSPI assured the Valley View administrative team that they would tackle the problems of legislation, pensions, and finance—all areas in which they were destined to give substantial and continuing help.

ASSEMBLY PASSES TWO BILLS

Ultimately the Office of the Superintendent of Public Instruction submitted two bills to the Illinois School Problems Commission (a joint, advisory legislative body):

1. House Bill 1525—which gave the OSPI discretionary powers in determining a new average daily attendance (ADA) formula for calculating State aid for schools operating on a year-round calendar. This act provided that a district would receive as much State aid per student as before, but no more. It was passed at the first session of the 76th General Assembly in 1969, and was signed into law by Governor Richard B. Ogilvie.

2. House Bill 529—an amendment to the 1964 "Year-Round School" bill, which would make it legal for an entire school district to go on a year-round calendar, provided that it met the minimum of 180 school days prescribed by the state code. Governor Ogilvie vetoed this bill, after the 1969 session of the Legislature recessed, on the recommendation of a staff advisor, David Sturgis, who contended that the legislation discriminated against districts which might want to test a year-round calendar in one or more schools in the district. (He was thinking primarily of Chicago and the middle-sized cities in the State, which would obviously want to test calendar revision in a few schools before committing an entire system.)

Governor Ogilvie's veto of House Bill 529 (in the summer of 1969) proved quite a traumatic experience to the Valley View administrators. By this time, however, they were so deeply committed to the 45-15 plan that they were determined to move ahead with it and brave a taxpayers' suit, if necessary. Ultimately, Governor Ogilvie was destined to approve a revised bill in the 1969 "rump" session of the 76th General Assembly. He traveled to Romeoville to sign the bill in the offices of District 96, the day before "Track A" entered the year-round school, June 29, 1970.

In October, 1968, the momentum of calendar revision was mounting rapidly. The District 96 administrators were venturing onto untested ground, without the benefit of the counsel or approval of their educational peers. The opportunity to "try out" 45-15 on other educators came October 22 and 23, at a year-round school conference sponsored by Dr. Ralph Belnap of the College of Education of Northern Illinois University, in DeKalb, Illinois.

The Valley View administrators were especially interested in this NIU conference, reports Jim Gove. "We thought, at last there was going to be a conference that we could go to, and find out what is happening about year-round school around the United States. We were quite disappointed. We were almost getting scared at that point, in that there was no year-round school in operation, that we could go and see, anywhere in the United States. There wasn't anybody we could go and ask, 'How is your plan working?' "

"AUTHORITIES"—OVERNIGHT

"We found a group of about 130 educators—local and county superintendents, principals and board members—all from Illinois. All were interested in the year-round school, but none had done any practical work on it. Mrs. Mary Liebman, a layman, of McHenry, Illinois, was one of the principal speakers, and outlined most of the theoretical plans that had been discussed during the debate of the past 15 years. Then the conference broke up into small working groups. Each of our four representatives attended a different discussion group.

"To our amazement, we found out that *we were the authorities.* That we were actually doing something about the year-round school, and were conversant with the problems and the pros and cons. We did get an opportunity to present our plan for criticism by other educators. We gave them every opportunity to pick it to pieces. Several administrators commented that we might have difficulty maintaining our buildings. Beyond that, none of the people in the group found anything wrong with our plan."

The Valley View administrators were invited to join in a panel the first evening of the conference, and were questioned at great length by the other educators. The discourse gave them confidence that they were on the right track and helped them to formulate answers to the various problems that they were going to face.

At the evening session the speaker was Robert M. Beckwith, manager, education department, Illinois State Chamber of Commerce, Chicago. Mr. Beckwith has been a prime mover in getting the Illinois Legislature to pass its bills favoring year-round schools and was to prove to be a one-man locomotive in moving the Legislature to update its year-round school code in 1969, and again in 1970 (after Governor Ogilvie vetoed one of the key enabling bills).

With the case for the 45-15 plan well-formulated as the result of the exposure at DeKalb, the Valley View administrators felt competent to take up their proposal formally with the leaders of the Romeoville and Bolingbrook communities.

The Valley View schools have traditionally taken their referendum requests and similar problems directly to voters in their homes. They have eschewed the familiar "Citizens' Advisory Committee," which has become a standard vehicle when school districts promote bond issues and tax rate increases.

This time, however, the administrators and the board members wanted to "try their ideas" out on as many leaders of the community as possible. Accordingly, the school board invited approximately 100 lay people to an open meeting on November 5, 1968. The invitation list included mayors, ministers, village trustees, parent-teacher organization officials, Jaycees, Kiwanians, Rotarians, Lions, and other service organization members. About 50 guests showed up, and listened intently, while the vice president of the board and the administrators explained the 45-15 plan. The school spokesmen did not attempt to "sell" the plan; rather they "explained it."

NO DOUBLE SHIFTS OR JUMBO CLASSES

The alternatives were presented:

To place a large part of District 96 on double shifts.

To increase the size of classes to as many as 40 students.

The members of the community already had experienced double shifts. The two-platoon system had been adopted temporarily several times before, while the district was waiting for contractors to finish up new buildings or additions. And classes had been increased to about 40 temporarily in some schools, awaiting completion of new quarters. The opposition was especially strong to the double-shift system, because it was then, and is now, being followed by Lockport West High School (then District 211 of Will County, and now a new, independent district). The Lockport high schools have had an extremely difficult time financially, politically and administratively, and have enjoyed poor public relations in the Valley View District, which they serve. The guests listened with great interest to the presentation, and spent considerable time inspecting Pat Page's 34-foot-long projected calendar for 1970-71. Questions were numerous.

90 PERCENT APPROVAL

Towards the end of the evening, Harold Lindstrom, then vice president of the Board of Education of District 96 and chairman of the meeting, asked the question that would either make the year-round school a success, or kill it. He asked, "How many of your community leaders here approve of the year-round school plan?" All but five of the fifty people present raised their hands, indicating approval. In the judgment of the administrators, the plan would have ended right then and there, without the approval of the community leaders.

Assured of backing by the community's leading spokesmen, and endorsed strongly by the Board of Education, the administrators proceeded to implement the program simultaneously on four separate fronts:

1. A full-scale information program to acquaint every family in the community with the school district's housing problem, and its proposed solution—the 45-15 Continuous School Plan.

2. A lobbying program with the General Assembly and its School Problems Commission in Springfield. In this campaign they were aided by Ray Page, State Superintendent of Public Instruction; Robert Beckwith, the Illinois State Chamber of Commerce; and the three Illinois Representatives and the Senator from the 41st Illinois Legislative District, which includes Will County.

3. Direct negotiations with the newly formed Valley View Educational Organization, a chapter of the Illinois Education Association, and the official negotiating body for the faculty.

4. Organizing the mechanics of 45-15—the scheduling of students, teachers, and classrooms; the organization of a flexible school busing system; and the evaluation of each step.

The next three chapters of this book will deal with the teacher negotiations, scheduling problems and solutions, and the response of children. The remainder of this chapter will be devoted, chronologically, to the community information campaign, and to winning support from the State and Federal officials.

19 MONTHS LEAD TIME

In discussing the community and public relations program, it must be kept in mind that the actual implementation of the 45-15 program was about 19 months away. The administrators began talking to the public intensively in November 1968. The first group of students was scheduled to enter the 45-15 plan on June 30, 1970. The authors wish to impress on the reader that at least this much "lead time" was necessary to work out the technicalities of scheduling, school census, air conditioning, curriculum adjustment (actually a minor problem), and teacher negotiations. These problems were in addition to passing, in two sessions of the Illinois Legislature, needed changes in the School Code. It is expected that other districts— certainly in Illinois —would not require that much time in the future, if the lessons from Valley View are heeded. (In fact, two districts, one in Vermont and one in Virginia, have successfully introduced the 45-15 plan in less than ten months.)

The public must be taken into the board's confidence, because it is neither practical nor moral to carry out extensive plans behind doors (illegal in Illinois, under the Scariano "open meetings" Act). Information is bound to leak out, and to be distorted or misunderstood. It was just plain common sense to keep the Community informed constantly and completely, and to insure full coverage of every decision in newspaper reports of Board of Education meetings.

Essentially, the Valley View information campaign was similar in many respects to the campaigns conducted by other school boards to "sell the public" on tax rate increases or authorization to issue bonds to finance school construction.

A "DIFFERENT" COMMUNICATIONS APPROACH

The Valley View campaign was "different" in two important essentials:

1. There was no formal or continuing "citizens' advisory committee." The District 96 board and administration believed then, and still believe, that the imposition of such an additional "super board" on top of a complex, major change in operations would merely complicate the job of maintaining Community confidence.

2. Instead, reliance was placed mainly on person-to-person contacts by a small team, composed of the superintendent of schools and one or more officers or members of the Board of Education.

This does not mean that the school system missed any opportunity to present the 45-15 story to any group, of any size, at any time. District 96 is one of those fortunate school districts in which the Community is interested and sends representatives to attend School Board meetings regularly. At every meeting, the president made a point of asking members of the audience to suggest, or to arrange, meetings with groups of any type or size. It is noteworthy that the superintendent of schools accepted 60 invitations to talk with small neighborhood groups (in addition to service clubs and churches) over a period of 18 months to explain the year-round school program.

The neighborhood meetings were literally "kaffee klatches." Ken Hermansen and a board member (frequently Lindstrom or Bingle) would call on the afternoon (or morning) host, carrying with them an electric coffee maker, disposable cups, and a selection of doughnuts or sweet rolls (all paid for by the School District). Ken was always careful to take off his shoes (like Dutch children). He would then sit in the middle of the floor, and with the help of the board members, play "At Random" with the invited guests, who might number anywhere from four or five up to a dozen.*

Questions were informal. The discussions would range over every aspect of the school system and its operations, and virtually every facet of education. Here the "gripes" and "worries" of individual parents over their children would come out in the open, giving the school administration a valuable opportunity to get constant "feedback" on the conduct of the schools. This "At Random" technique has been followed by Hermansen and the school board for years, and has been a major contributing factor to the Board of Education's success in securing public endorsement in seven referendums. A big help in these meetings was Pat Page's four-color calendar of the "Valley View 45-15 Plan," (See foldout opposite page 84) which was reduced from the 34-foot long accordion-fold display presented at large meetings to a single sheet that every family can tack up in its kitchen. With this chart, every parent can tell at a glance on what days schools are to be closed, and on what days each school "quarter" will begin and end.

MULTIMEDIA TOOLS

The four-color chart was only one of many audio-visual tools that were employed to present the 45-15 plan graphically to the com-

---

*"At Random" is the name of a popular, informal "talk" program broadcast for many years by WBBM-TV, the CBS television outlet in Chicago.

munity. There was a set of overhead transparencies, which presented the financial-housing plight of the school system. There was also a 15-minute audio-visual presentation, consisting of a series of color slides, and a tape-recorded narration by a teacher who "moonlights" as a radio announcer over a Joliet station. This tape presentation was used especially for formal meetings, such as service clubs and PTO's. It has turned out to be extremely useful to the hundreds of school administrators and board members who have visited the Valley View schools since 45-15 has received national publicity. The visitors are seated in a small conference room, while one administrator turns on the slide-tape show. Usually most of their basic questions are answered before they begin their formal interviews.

PRESS-RADIO-TV

The local community newspapers in Romeoville, Bolingbrook, Joliet, Lockport, Naperville, and Chicago, have been of inestimable value in keeping the parents of School District 96 informed of the plan as it has progressed. Almost from the start, Chicago's four daily metropolitan newspapers have devoted large space to describing the plan, and to reporting its implementation as "D" day neared. These reports gave confidence to the administrators and assurance to the community. Robert Beckwith, of the Illinois State Chamber of Commerce, played no small role in winning national attention for the Valley View 45-15 Continuous School Plan. The ISCC distributed bulletins to the press nationwide in January of 1970 and in January of 1971. These releases have won a substantial volume of favorable editorial comment, as well as coverage in syndicated columns and on both local TV stations and national TV networks. As the result of this national attention, the Valley View superintendent's office has received approximately 100 inquiries from other school systems each week since January 1970. To service these inquiries, and to otherwise communicate the findings at Valley View to other interested school districts, District 96 has requested, and has obtained, a special "Dissemination Grant" from the Illinois Superintendent of Public Instruction.

DIAL FOR ANSWERS

An interesting sidelight on the public relations program is the District's use of Illinois Bell Telephone Company's "Dial a Message"

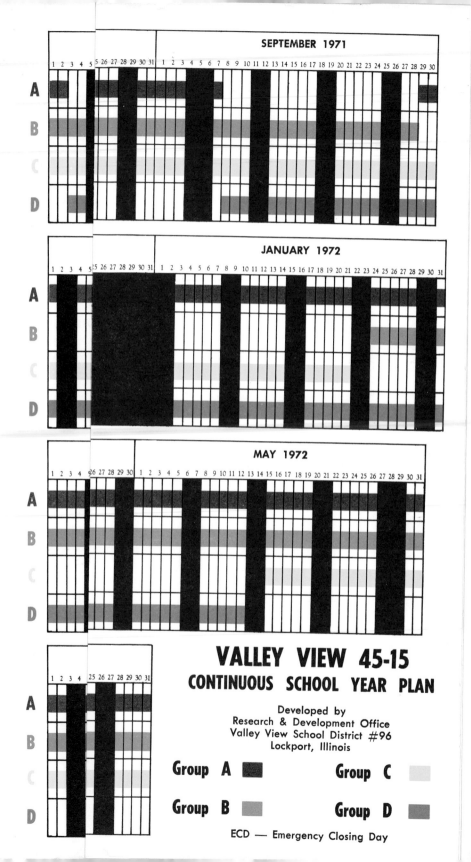

VALLEY VIEW 45-15
CONTINUOUS SCHOOL YEAR PLAN

Developed by
Research & Development Office
Valley View School District #96
Lockport, Illinois

Group A

Group B

Group C

Group D

ECD — Emergency Closing Day

Valley View School District No. 96

DALHART AVENUE, VILLAGE OF ROMEOVILLE
P. O. LOCKPORT, ILLINOIS 60441

December 26, 1969

The Doe Family
360 Maple Lane
Lockport, Illinois

Dear Parent:

School District No. 96 will be enrolling some 1500 additional students for this coming school year. Our classrooms, however, are already overcrowded even though we have built as many schools as we are financially permitted to build at this time.

Your Board of Education is determined to continue to provide the best possible educational experiences for elementary-grade children. If providing classroom facilities under a conventional school year calendar is no longer possible, a new approach to scheduling is needed. The Board of Education and school administration have prepared and adopted a plan that will provide the classroom space we must have.

The schools will be kept open and operating all year long under a plan called the "Valley View 45-15 Plan". It will go into effect in the summer of 1970. This letter is being sent now so that your family activities for the coming year can take full advantage of the opportunities of the new school calendar.

In your particular family, children will begin the next school year on June 30, 1970. All holidays and vacations are shown on the enclosed calendar through August, 1971.

You will receive more information in the coming months — about school busses, school attendance sites and registering children who will begin school for the first time. We promise to keep you fully informed of any detail of the new schedule that may affect your family in any way.

With best wishes for the remainder of this holiday season, I remain,

Sincerely,

Kenneth Hermansen

Kenneth Hermansen
Superintendent of Schools

GROUP "A" - "Red Bar"
Start of 1970 - 1971 school year   June 30, 1970
End of 1970 - 1971 school year   June 2, 1971
Vacation periods: June 11, 1970 thru June 29, 1970
        September 1, 1970 thru September 22, 1970
        November 28, 1970 thru December 27, 1970 (includes Christmas
                                                   school closing)
        March 3, 1971 thru March 23, 1971
        April 3, 1971 thru April 11, 1971 (Easter school closing)
        June 3, 1971 thru July 5, 1971 (includes summer school closing)
        Plus all Illinois legal school closing holidays (in black)
July 6, 1971 - Start of second school year under the Valley
        View 45-15 Continuous School Year Plan

FIGURE 2. Just before Christmas, 1969, every family in the Valley View School District 96 received this letter, along with a typed list of the grade assignment and 45-15 starting date for the children in their family. All children in each family started with the same "track," on the same date. The letter and the accompanying list were produced by computer.

the following June 30?" There was no need for fear. None of the principals, administrators, and board members received any communications during the 10-day Christmas holiday. When the school offices reopened January 5, there were two derogatory letters and two derogatory phone calls from parents. Approximately 25 parents inquired whether their families could be shifted to different "tracks" or groups because of personal vacation plans or other (business) reasons. These requests were granted without exception, since they made up such a tiny proportion of the September, 1970 enrollment, 6,603 students. The information campaign had been a complete success.

SCHOOL BOARD UNOPPOSED

The School Board enjoyed another opportunity to appraise the community's response to 45-15 on April 11, 1970, school election day. There were two vacancies on the board of education, due to transfers of incumbent members. Two former board members were nominated for the vacancies. There were no other candidates nominated, and there were no write-in votes, opposing the nominees on election day. The administration felt that if there were any opposition to the plan, it would have been expressed at this school board election.

The voters had an additional opportunity to express any dissatisfaction with 45-15 on August 15, 1970—six weeks after children began attending classes under the plan. By a substantial majority they approved three propositions—an $835,000 bond issue, a $1,700,000 "interest free" loan from the Illinois Building Commission, and an increase in the educational tax rate.

Things were also progressing well on the Legislative front. The Valley View administrators had "panicked" during the summer of 1969, when Governor Ogilvie vetoed House Bill 529, the year-round school law. Robert Beckwith of ISCC happened to be in Springfield at the time and assured the Valley View people that the veto was based on one fault in the bill—that it did not give large school systems the authority to institute year-round school programs in less than the entire district. This fault was remedied in a new bill, which was submitted at a special "rump" session of the 76th General Assembly in March, 1970. The revised bill was passed swiftly by both houses of the legislature before the special session adjourned. However, it lay on Governor Ogilvie's desk, unsigned until June 29, 1970—the day before students in "Group A" were scheduled to begin their first 45 day school session. On that day the Governor journeyed from Springfield to Romeoville and signed the bill, seated at an old-fashioned school desk which had been salvaged from one of District 96's original one room schoolhouses. This action focused attention of the Chicago metropolitan newspapers and television stations on 45-15, providing another vehicle for intensive publicity coverage. Present at the signing were officials of District 96; Ray Page, Superintendent of Public Instruction, and officials of the Illinois State Chamber of Commerce, which had assisted in securing Legislative approval for the year-round school. (See figs. 3 and 4.)

FIGURE 3. State, local and business officials visited Valley View School District 96 administration offices on June 29, 1970, day before the 45-15 Continuous School plan was placed in operation officially. Posing for a formal photograph are Kenneth L. Hermansen, superintendent; William J. Crowley, then president of the Illinois State Chamber of Commerce and now chairman of the new U.S. Postal Rate Commission; James Bingle, president of School District 96; Governor Richard B. Ogilvie; Ray Page, then State Superintendent of Public Instruction; and Alwin C. Aigner, chairman of the ISCC education committee.

FIGURE 4. "It's a law!" Governor Richard B. Ogilvie of Illinois, waves a copy of the new Illinois Year-Round School law for television cameras as state, local and business officials look on. He is seated at an old-fashioned school "bench" salvaged from the original, one room Valley View School.

9

Teachers

A school is only as good as its teachers. From the first days of considering the year-round school, the Valley View administration recognized that the confidence of and co-operation by, the teachers was essential to the success of the program. As mentioned earlier, the teachers were informed of the program long before any decisions were made; in fact before any recommendations were made to the Board of Education. Ken Hermansen first discussed the possibility of the year-round school at a District teachers' workshop in April, 1968. At that time he had no particular plan in mind, only a vague recognition that some form of calendar reform would prove a key to solving the District's student housing problem.

Hermansen explained to the teachers that students would not attend school all year. Rather, he pointed out, they would attend school 180 days, with class days and vacations rotating in an unconventional pattern. The teachers were informed that they would probably have an option of working only 180 days a year, or that they might work 245 days or more. They were told, also, that they would not be penalized in their salary for working a summer schedule, as is common in many optional summer school programs. It was suggested that teachers would enjoy more flexibility in pursuing advanced professional education.

OVERCOMING TEACHER DISTRUST

The problem of teacher communications was a delicate one. The Valley View Education Association was participating for the first time in professional and salary negotiations with the administration and the Board of Education. Initially there was distrust. The year 1967-68 was one in which teachers generally were becoming relatively militant and anxious to wipe out many of the economic disadvantages, which they felt made them second class citizens. Naturally, they were apprehensive about the impact of any radical calendar change on their working habits and rewards. Because a comprehensive contract was being negotiated for the first time, and because District 96—a relatively poor district—was lagging behind some of the more prosperous districts southwest and south of Chicago, negotiations for the 1968-69 school year dragged out until September, when the School Board is required by law to file its budget and tax levy ordinance for the coming fiscal year.

To insure that teachers were well informed and amenable to the proposed 45-15 Continuous School Year Plan, three measures were taken:

1. Ronald Strahonoski, a teacher, was assigned to assist John Lukancik, assistant superintendent, as director of curriculum. Although both Hermansen and Lukancik joined with members of the Board negotiating committee in all discussions with the education association representatives, Strahonoski was given the full time assignment of informing the faculty on the proposed changes and keeping two-way channels of communications open.

2. A teachers' committee of representatives from each school building in the District was formed. These teachers were paid $5 an hour for participating in committee meetings and for all other time they devoted to helping develop and implement the 45-15 program. Their job was to supplement and assist the activity of the principals in relation to information and communications, and, particularly, to get and relay the answers to questions raised by faculty members. The work of this committee was invaluable.

3. A comprehensive, seven-page fact sheet, containing answers to 27 key questions, was developed and was distributed to all teachers along with their handbooks and professional contract material.

This fact sheet gave simple, direct, carefully constructed answers to all questions. Among them were such concerns as the 45-15 calendar, air conditioning, after-school activities, consecutive teaching and "lock step" teaching schedules, storage of teacher materials and transfer of materials to new classrooms on "back to school" days, rights to switch to another track, payment of teachers "on vacation" as substitutes, and effects of the program on teacher pay, retirement fund, and other benefits.

CHANNELS SPIKE RUMORS

The effectiveness of this chain of communication was demonstrated when Governor Ogilvie vetoed one of the two special bills the Legislature had passed to make the 45-15 program legal in Illinois. Rumors circulated the buildings quickly, and the questions were referred immediately to Ron Strahonoski. Cancellation of the year-round school program at the time would have affected seriously the plans of some teachers for the ensuing school year. The assurances of representatives of the Office of the State Superintendent of Public Instruction, and other Springfield legislative contacts, were passed on in a special bulletin. The concerns vanished.

In March, 1970, a full-scale teachers' "institute" was held to make sure that all members of the staff understood all of the ramifications of the 45-15 plan and their roles in implementing it. The atmosphere was interested and cordial, and there were few questions. The session demonstrated that the faculty had been developed into an aggressive team, eager to participate in their new adventure.

TABLE I

TEACHER SALARY SCHEDULE FOR 1970-1971 (184 DAYS)

	B.A.	+10 140	+20 150	M.A.	+15 175	2nd MA or CAS
0	7200	7300	7400	7700	7900	8100
1	7428	7535	7641	7961	8174	8387
2	7535	7641	7748	8121	8334	8547
3	7748	7854	7961	8387	8600	8813
4	7961	8067	8174	8653	8866	9079
5	8174	8280	8387	8919	9132	9345
6	8493	8600	8706	9292	9505	9718
7	8706	8813	8919	9558	9771	9984
8	8919	9026	9132	9825	10,038	10,251
9	9132	9239	9345	10,091	10,304	10,517
10	9345	9452	9558	10,357	10,570	10,783
11	9771	9878	9984	10,783	10,996	11,209
12	9984	10,091	10,197	10,996	11,209	11,433
13		10,304	10,410	11,209	11,433	11,635
14		10,517	10,623	11,433	11,635	11,848
15			10,836	11,688	11,848	12,061
16			11,369	12,168	12,381	12,594
20	10,197	10,730	11,582	12,381	12,594	12,807
25			11,795	12,700	12,900	13,200

NEGOTIATIONS COMPLETED EARLY

One of the special benefits of this extensive campaign of "listening and talking" with teachers was the outcome of salary negotiations for the 1970-71 school fiscal year. Most questions of professional policy had been ironed out the previous year. An agreement on salaries was reached in early June. This was three months before the deadline, and three months earlier than the previous year.

The base salary for a teacher with a bachelor's degree and certificate, and no experience was $7,200. This was approximately $600 lower than the base point on the "salary guides" of some of the more affluent suburbs nearby to the North. The authors do not intend to imply that the faculty accepted a lower scale than some of their neighbors because of the 45-15 plan. Rather, it reflects the teachers' understanding that District 96 is a "poor" district and that it had already reached the limit. Table I contains the annual salary guide approved in the 1970-71 contract with the faculty. Table II shows the "daily rate," obtained by dividing the annual salary by 180 days.

TABLE II
TEACHER SALARY SCHEDULE FOR 1970-1971 (DAILY RATE)

	B.A.	+10 140	+20 150	M.A.	+15 175	2nd MA or CAS
0	39.13	39.67	40.22	41,85	42.93	44.02
1	40.37	40.95	41.53	43.27	44.42	45.58
2	40.95	41.53	42.11	44.14	45.29	46.45
3	42.11	42.68	43.27	45.58	46.74	47.90
4	43.27	43.84	44.42	47.03	48.18	49.34
5	44.42	45.00	45.58	48.47	49.63	50.79
6	46.16	46.74	47.32	50.50	51.66	52.82
7	47.32	47.90	48.47	51.95	53.10	54.26
8	48.47	49.05	49.63	53.40	54.55	55.71
9	49.63	50.21	50.79	54.84	56.00	57.16
10	50.79	51.37	51.95	56.29	57.45	58.60
11	53.10	53.68	54.26	58.60	59.76	60.92
12	54.26	54.84	55.42	59.76	60.92	62.14
13		56.00	56.58	60.92	62.16	63.23
14		57.16	57.73	62.14	63.23	64.39
15			58.89	63.52	64.39	65.55
16			61.79	66.13	67.29	68.45
20	55.42	58.32	62.95	67.29	68.45	69.60
25			64.10	69.02	70.11	71.74

This schedule of daily rates made it easy for teachers to compute their income, if they worked more than the traditional school year, or if they substituted during "vacation days." The average 1970-71 salary for teachers in the District is $10,033.60.

TEACHERS PICK WORK YEARS

At all times, members of the faculty understood that they could elect a work year of their own choice. There were interesting patterns as the result. (See fig. 5.)

Primary teachers are generally younger than those in the intermediate and junior high grades. The proportion of females to males is

FIGURE 5. John Lukancik, assistant superintendent of schools for District 96, developed this graphic planning chart with magnetic symbols to keep track of the contract expiration and notification dates for individual teachers, as well as their vacation periods. The light colored metal tabs on the lower "Valley View" chart show the high proportion of primary teachers following the "lockstep" schedule of 45 days in school and 15 off, exactly the same as that of their students.

also higher. For the 1970-71 school year, 61.3 percent of the primary grade teachers elected to work 184 days—the regular school year (including teachers' workshops). Some 25.3 percent of the teachers elected to work 244 days—the year round schedule. The remainder of the primary teachers (13.3 percent) worked 199, 214, or 229 days, fitting in substitute work and adjusting their vacation plans to their own educational patterns. Some of these "between" teachers worked neither 184 nor 244 days because they joined the system as various "tracks" or "groups" entered school during the summer of 1970.

In discussing the primary teachers, it is important to note that all but six of the first grade teachers in the entire Valley View system elected to contract for 184 days, teaching 45 days and taking 15 days off for vacation, along with their pupils. This then gave almost all first grade children the attention from a single teacher that many educators consider important at this age. In two of the schools cooperative groups of four teachers were assigned to groups of first grade classes, giving a high measure of continuity for the beginners. The Valley View administrators feel, however, that educators tend to overrate the value of attachment to a single teacher in the first grade. They reason that the first graders meet many people in their lives— father, mother, grandfather, grandmother, aunt, uncle, milkman, mailman, and grocer. It is not necessary to isolate first graders from all contact with adults other than their primary classroom teacher.

In the intermediate grades, 40.8 percent of the teachers worked 244 days; 18.4 percent, 229 days; 22.4 percent, 184 days, and the remaining 13.2 percent worked for various periods between.

In junior high school, the shift to the longer work year is dramatic. Some 31.4 percent of the junior high teachers elected to work 274 days; 1.9 percent 254 days; and 16.6 percent for 244 days. There were 29.6 percent working 229 days and 1.9 percent working 234 days. Only 11.1 percent of the junior high school teachers worked 184 days—the traditional school year. The wide variance in the number of days work is primarily the result of different teaching loads in different special subjects in junior high. There were 27 different contract terms in all.

A breakdown of teacher contracts by sex is also interesting. More than half of the female teachers in the entire District elected to work the traditional 184 days, while only 20.6 percent worked 244 days or more. Only 6.5 percent of the male teachers worked a 184-day school year. There were 22.1 percent working 229 days, and 61.1 percent working 244 days or longer.

It is apparent from this analysis that the 45-15 plan is working to the tremendous economic advantage of male teachers—enabling them to work the year-round at their chosen profession, and allowing them to remain in teaching instead of being lured to a permanent non-teaching job that started as a vacation fill-in.

All kindergarten teachers were placed on a straight 184-day teaching schedule, assigned to supervising two shifts—morning and afternoon—with a total of approximately 1,200 kindergarten students registered in the District.

An interesting development among teachers in the primary grades was what we call "co-operative teaching," somewhat akin to the innovative "team teaching" system that has become increasingly prevalent at the junior high school level in recent years. In the Valley View "co-op teaching" plan, four teachers, each working the traditional 184-day year, will assume responsibility for four groups of students—rotating every 60 days, but maintaining continuity in their curriculum. The students get to know all four teachers when they trade rooms on special occasions, and this makes the transition easier. The majority of the primary teachers, however, teach "lock step." That is, they teach 45 days, and take 15 days off for vacation, just as the children do. This gives the primary grade children the same teacher for the full year as in the traditional school calendar system. It also gives the teacher a pause to refresh, and "charge her batteries," every 60 days.

QUARTERLY REFRESHERS

The reports the administration gets back from teachers indicate that the teachers actually look forward to this quarterly vacation, which gives them a keen anticipation of relief from the admittedly great pressures of handling 28 six-, seven-, or eight-year-old children.

Dr. William M. Rogge, professor of education at the University of Illinois, Urbana, distributed a base-line questionnaire to all of the members of the professional staff of District 96 on June 9, 1970—three weeks before the first group of students was scheduled to enter the first 45-15 school year. The teachers filled out questionnaires as one of several parts of a "Case Study of the Valley View

District 45-15 Plan" funded by the Bureau of Research, Office of Education, U.S. Department of Health, Education and Welfare.

These interviews, along with similar studies of opinion from members of the Valley View Community and comprehensive educational testing of sample groups of students, will form the foundation for a three-year evaluation of the educational import of the 45-15 program. (This base study is described in more detail in Chapter 13.)

The teachers, on June 9, completed 161 questionnaires. Dr. Rogge reports that only a small percentage of the staff showed mild or strong objections to the plan. The largest percentage involved (twelve percent) expressed the opinion that the 45-15 plan would not be in operation in five years. On the other hand, a majority (59 percent) said they mildly or heartily agreed with the statement that ". . . the 45-15 plan is the most exciting educational innovation I have ever participated in."

The members of the faculty were less certain about student learning under the 45-15 plan. About 43 percent thought students would learn more because of several short vacations being substituted for one long summer vacation. More than half (56 percent) agreed that a higher proportion of male teachers would compose the faculty in five years. About a third (29 percent) thought that teachers would become "tired or worn out" if they taught 244 days. More than a third (39 percent) thought that families in the community would get used to the short vacation and would give mild or strong support to the plan after a year.

It is hard to quantify the impact of 45-15 on the faculty, however. The administrators had so many problems of planning, scheduling, housing, community relations, and faculty negotiations that they could not initiate or supervise a comprehensive look at the impact of the 45-15 plan on the curriculum.

CURRICULUM INNOVATION INSPIRED

Ken Hermansen has always followed a "permissive" or "democratic" policy on innovation. "We don't try to impose innovation down from the top," he reports. "However, we do everything we can to encourage creative innovation by members of the faculty at all levels."

According to John Lukancik, the administration foresaw "no great upheaval in curriculum" as the result of the 45-15 plan. "We had no quarters or semesters," Lukancik recalls. "Students were given passing grades at the end of the year. However, parents were accustomed to receiving grade reports at the end of nine, eighteen, and twenty seven weeks. It just happened that nine weeks include 45 teaching days, and there was somewhat of a natural break at that time."

However, the faculty didn't follow the expected pattern. Teachers, like administrators, are concerned greatly with "individualization of instruction." They see the 45-day vacation break as the logical point marking a complete quarter or unit of instruction. Teachers reported that they are always reluctant to "fail" a student at the end of a year. But the 45-day mark might prove an opportune time for a student to transfer to another group or "track" to repeat necessary material for a few weeks. It might also prove an opportune time to accelerate the exceptional student.

Jamie McGee, chairman of the mathematics department and president of the Valley View Education Association, points out that the 15-day vacation break offers a logical spot for tutoring or "catch up" work that will enable the slow learner to be promoted with his class.

According to McGee, who was released from teaching assignments for curriculum development in mathematics during the 1970-71 year, the members of the math faculty have taken the initiative in an entire restructuring and individualization of the mathematics curriculum, catalyzed, to some extent by the ferment of 45-15.

"We can't just start to say that come next July 6, at the start of the 1971-72 school year, everything will be individualized. But that is the ultimate goal," McGee comments. "In the past we haven't studied the kids enough. We have just accepted them where they were, in fourth, or sixth, or eighth grade. Then we attempted to cram into them what the textbook author considered to be the quantum of knowledge that a fourth, sixth, or eighth grade student should have. In the future, we are going to try to find out where the student is, and then to fit him into the group in which he will perform and relate more easily. We believe that the 45-15 plan gives the faculty a new level of flexibility in individualizing its teaching, and relating it to the students' real needs."

Technically, Valley View has for some years followed the "ungraded school" philosophy—at least in the "tracking" of primary youngsters in reading, language arts, and arithmetic. In Hermansen's opinion, the first year's experience with 45-15 has opened the door to full utilization of the "ungraded school" concept. In fact, Valley View's next building, Oak View School, being built in the Indian Oaks sector of Bolingbrook, will be a "school without walls." The kindergarten and remedial reading students will be separated from the rest of the six grades by moveable partitions. The remainder of the primary and intermediate students will move freely in time and space throughout a wall-less building. But that's another story, to be told in Chapter 14.

10

Systems

Most year-round school proposals advanced since 1930 have foundered on three problems:

1. Difficulty (or fear of difficulty) in communicating the need and the merits of the proposed solution to the community—especially the four staggered quarter plan, which required turning one fourth of the students out of school for a three month winter "vacation."

2. Inertia on the part of administrators and teachers, who enjoyed the "status quo," which offered three months for vacation, study, or moonlighting in the summer.

3. Genuine concern with the exceedingly complex problem of scheduling a large number of students into the available underpopulated classrooms, to secure even, full utilization of school buildings—the primary goal of most year-round school proposals.

In previous chapters, we have discussed the solutions to the first two problems—communications, and faculty-administrator relations.

This chapter is devoted to the third—scheduling of an entire elementary school district by computer and to related problems of transportation and maintenance scheduling, often raised by the hundreds of school administrators and school board members who have visited Valley View since 45-15 went into effect.

The Valley View administrators were aware that considerable progress had been made in using electronic computers to schedule students, faculty and classrooms in colleges and high schools such as Lewis College, a private (Catholic) technical institute, located in the Valley View District only two miles from the administrative offices. We knew that we could use the Lewis computer on a "leased or shared" time basis, and that we might not necessarily need to purchase or lease a computer full time. (Ultimately, with other considerations, such as student record-keeping in mind, District 96 did lease a small computer, capable of filling its business office needs.)

On the first visit to the Office of the State Superintendent of Public Instruction in October 1968, Hermansen requested that the state agency help solve the especially complex scheduling problem that full utilization of classrooms, buses, faculty and other facilities required.

REQUIREMENTS DEFINED

"Donald Norwood of the OSPI asked us to specify our needs so that he and his computer staff could work on the problem," Hermansen reports. "We explained our idea of the 45-15 plan and mentioned that we wanted all children from the same family, and from the same immediate neighborhood, on the same schedule, if possible. Norwood replied that he understood the problem and that he would try to help if we could formulate our specific requirements. However, it soon became clear to us, and to them, that the OSPI data processing staff had neither the expertise nor the time to attack our scheduling problems. Norwood said, however, that he would scout around the data processing 'fraternity.' "

In December, 1968, Hermansen received a visit from Stanley Patton and Robert Norfleet, then members of the Educational Services Division of Compumatics, Inc., a Chicago data processing system firm. Compumatics' Educational Services Division was then headed by Dr. Benjamin Willis, former general superintendent of the Chicago Public Schools, former president of the American Association of School Administrators, and now superintendent of Broward County Schools in Fort Lauderdale, Florida. (Incidentally, the Broward County Schools are currently working on year-round school 'enrichment' programs at the Nova High School, a county-wide institution that has won considerable national attention.) Compumatics was given the opportunity to make a proposal to District 96 in January.

The district also considered proposals from Statistical Tabulating Company, probably the nation's largest independent tabulating service bureau, and Honeywell, one of the larger computer manufacturers. Statab proposed sending in programmers with a systems background to study our problem in depth. Honeywell's representatives seemed to be concerned primarily with selling us "hardware," which we were anxious at the time to avoid buying.

Compumatics' Educational Services Division offered more pertinent services, and considerable educational background, including that of Dr. Willis. In February, the Board of Education approved signing a contract with Compumatics to survey the district's scheduling problem and related systems.

The Compumatics executive assigned to study our problem was Bob Norfleet, a gifted school system analyst, who had topped off experience in private industry with considerable time in the systems division of the Chicago Public Schools. At the time he headed Chicago's Systems department, it had the largest educational data processing installation outside of the nation's colleges and universities. His experience proved to be valuable in the much smaller, but painstakingly detailed, problem environment of the Valley View 45-15 school system. Norfleet was assigned the task of stating the School District's scheduling and operating requirements, and then preparing a report that detailed the systems and procedures to be followed in assigning pupils and teachers to classrooms and in efficient utilization of buses and other resources. He was destined to spend more than half his time at Valley View during the next two years, contributing materially to minimizing the administrative headaches that 45-15 might have presented. He also participated in a federally sponsored feasibility study of the 45-15 plan adopted by the Valley View Schools. This chapter is devoted primarily to the scheduling requirements and the systems solutions arrived at in Valley View, largely through Norfleet's efforts.

Many readers will be familiar with the use of computers by colleges and universities to schedule students, teachers and classrooms during registration periods. The Valley View problem was somewhat related, although there are extra time and distance factors introduced by the fact that there are eight elementary school buildings, four distinct groups or "tracks" of students, and close to 300 identifiable neighborhoods from which the groups are drawn.

Actually, at Valley View, the systems crew had to produce a schedule in December 1969—six months before the students were to enter the first group of 45-15 cycles. In addition, the schedule had to be planned to take into that schedule all children who were to enter the district, at all age levels, between June 30, 1970, and the end of June 1971. The trick was one of handling a dynamic student enrollment situation within the parameters of static classrooms and teacher contracts.

The schedule task, in a way, was to play with assistance from the computer a giant "war game" like the familiar Battleship or Tic-Tac-Toe, which are played with pencil and paper. Before the authors get into explaining the operation of their "war game," however, they should give the reader a clear statement of the problems that needed solving.

COMPREHENSIVE RECORDS

The end goal of the entire scheduling process is a set of printed "class lists" that provide the building principals with the names, ages, phone numbers, addresses and parents' names of the children assigned to each class. These class lists reflected the hours of planning that guaranteed full utilization of every classroom available in every building, and for full utilization of all twenty school buses, all year long. Each class list represents a group of students assigned to:

A school site
An attendance group or cycle (A, B, C, or D)
A grade level
A teaching position (or home room).

The reader must remember, also, that the systems analyst and the computer are dealing with a precious commodity—kids. No end of harm can happen by sending a child to a classroom without a seat, by rescheduling him to a group that has a different vacation time than his brothers, sisters and neighbors, by sending him to the wrong building, or by providing his parents with the wrong bus schedule.

There were a number of other important requirements:

1. Each individual family must receive a school schedule which showed clearly the attendance cycle and the vacation days for each pupil in the family. It is reasonable that parents need this information six months ahead of the day school starts to plan vacations.

2. It was important that the central district administration office and each school principal be able to locate any pupil in the district at any time. To fail in this respect would lead to bad public relations. It was important for the superintendent to have a master list showing the positions of the entire student population.

3. When 45-15 plan started up, it was necessary to transfer a number of children from one building to another, to balance out occupancy, and to insure that they be housed at the closest school offering space. This, then, required a master list for each "sending" school, telling when and where to transfer each student's records.

4. The district office also needed a report by site, grade, and attendance cycle in order to assign qualified teachers.

5. Provision had to be made at Valley View Junior High School to fulfill the individual elections of each student. (This part of the job is similar to college class scheduling.) However, the scheduling process had to place these children in the proper group (A, B, C, or D), so that they would have the same vacation periods as the other members of their families, and their neighbors.

6. The district office needed regular summary reports showing the current utilization of every room and every building, including the number of seats available for children moving into the district.

7. The transportation director needed a list of pupils to be transported to each site, from each of 263 neighborhoods, in each group, and at each hour (the buses make several runs each morning and afternoon).

8. A more traditional by-product required was production, from time to time, of current lists of students, or index cards, for use in attendance reporting, tests, and classroom grades.

COMMUNITY CONSIDERATIONS

The systems analyst also defined three other parameters, or constraints, that would take into consideration those requirements imposed by the community, those by educational objectives, and those related chiefly to administrative policy and procedures. These constraints were not necessarily mutually exclusive; they merely were broken down into these three categories, to create a more manageable chore. Here, for example, are some of the community restraints that were to affect the scheduling process:

1. Pupils in a single family should be on the same attendance cycle. (That is they should start school and vacation on the same day.)

2. Pupils in the same neighborhood should be on the same attendance cycle. The concern here, in addition to bus scheduling, was to enable parents to know when to expect other children on the streets during the three-week vacations.

3. Kindergarten and primary pupils living within walking distance of a school site should attend that school.

4. A pupil should attend the same school all year long.

5. Future community recreational and similar programs should be co-ordinated with the "at home" three weeks of children in each neighborhood.

EDUCATIONAL REQUIREMENTS

Some of the educational considerations follow:

1. Kindergarten pupils should attend on a two-shift basis.

2. Pupils who meet minimum starting age restrictions in September should be allowed to start school in July.

3. The "ungraded" system in the three primary grades should be maintained.

4. Elementary classroom size should approximate 28 and junior high school size approximate 32 to assure "capacity" utilization. (This would enable the school district to meet the "emergency" standards required to secure financing for additional buildings from the Illinois School Building Commission.)

5. Junior high school pupils should continue to have "electives" and individual scheduling.

6. Primary classes should have the same teacher for a full year, if possible.

7. Time should be provided for extra-curricular activities, regardless of cycle.

ADMINISTRATIVE NEEDS

Among the purely administrative considerations were these:

1. Classrooms should be utilized fully all year.

2. Variations in class size between different parts of the district should be minimized.

3. A school site should have the same attendance boundary for all grades attending that school.

4. Teacher preferences for grade, course and building assignments should be respected as much as possible.

5. Pupil transportation costs should be minimized.

6. Provisions should be made for extra-curricular activities.

In the systems study it was determined that the 45-15 plan would effectively reduce the number of classrooms needed in the primary and intermediate grades (K-6) from 161 classrooms to 124 classrooms. Sample schedules were prepared at an early date (March 1969) for all of the existing elementary buildings, the two new elementary buildings to be built, and the West View Junior High School, which was already being utilized to more than rated capacity. It was determined that the 45-15 plan would permit West View to house 1,349 students, in comparison with 1,230 students estimated for the fall of 1971. This information alone (obtained from a simulated scheduling) made it possible to defer an immediate addition to West View or construction of a second junior high school at an early date.

On the basis of his preliminary systems analysis, Norfleet reported that the 45-15 plan offered more potential than other year-round rotating programs. He stated, without qualification, that the plan has "exceptional merit, educationally, administratively, and socially."

THREE CRITICAL POINTS

Norfleet predicted that the plan would face critical test of survival at three points:

1. Acceptance by the teachers. "An organized teacher protest," he said, "would put you out of business."

2. The date on which parents would be notified formally of their childrens' assignments. (Just before Christmas in 1969.)

3. The first 120 days of operation of the plan—mostly between June 30, 1970, and Christmas of the same year.

CONSULTANTS FALLIBLE

Educators, as well as businessmen, who have utilized consultants will be interested in one aspect of Norfleet's recommendations. He insisted emphatically that all students should enter the 45-15 program on the same date, June 30, 1970. Otherwise, he held, the parents of the first group (A) would feel that they were being imposed upon because their children would have only three weeks of vacation before starting school. The plan of bringing everyone in on June 30 required some schedule juggling, which the consultant provided. Also, he said, it would give everyone a chance to catch his breath, and to adjust to the 45-15 plan's shortcomings in November and December. However, the recommendation was not accepted.

"I kept predicting doom," Norfleet recalls. "At least a picket line of 'A' mothers. . . . The results were hardly what I expected. The 'A' group came to school peacefully, and the effect on the school staff was excellent. July was a welcome month of 'phasing in.' " Norfleet now agrees that the first summer's calendar was appropriate for the Valley View schools and community even though contrary to his strong recommendations.

The consultant completed by March 24, 1969, a preliminary schedule for utilization of all of the buildings in the district. This confirmed that everyone could be accommodated in the 1970-71 school year but that an additional building would probably be required by 1971-72.

"LEAD TIME" MAPPED OUT

He also set out a tentative "timetable" for completing the various systems jobs that needed to be done to bring children into the 45-15 continuous plan by June 30, 1970. Here were the target dates, submitted to, and approved by the Board of Education:

1969

April	—Plot tentative school boundaries for 45-15 Plan.
	—Prepare for census.
May	—Take census and compile results.
	—Prepare detailed housing projections.
June	—Revise tentative school boundaries.
	—Prepare classroom plans and alternatives for three and eight year periods.
	—Build control maps of the district.
October	—Prepare student and class information for scheduling.
November	—Determine pupil cycles and sites for 45-15 and notify parents and teachers.
December	—Begin teacher assignment

1970

| April | —Begin kindergarten and first grade pre-enrollment. |
| May | —Produce class lists and other printouts for pupils in grades two through eight. |

The target dates for implementation of the plan in 1970 were established:

> June 11—Last day of 1969-70 school year
> June 30—First day of classes for 1970-71 school year, grades one through eight
> Sept. 1—First day of kindergarten.

PLANNING A CENSUS

Business managers and other administrators may be interested to know that the initial systems feasibility study cost the district approximately $8,000, while the additional work of the systems consultant for the following 15 months totaled $15,700. Added to the professional fees, of course, were the out-of-pocket costs of:

> Canvassers to complete the needed school census
> Clerical assistance in organizing the census data
> School staff to assist in pre-registration (which the school District would have incurred in any event)
> School staff to assist in pupil data collection and verification
> Continued staff assistance from the research director, on approximately a half-time basis.
> Actual keypunching costs
> Actual computer time costs.

The first major task in preparing for the changeover to 45-15 was a complete and accurate census of the district. The census recorded, for each household, the name and address of the family, and the name, sex, and birth date of each child. The census questionnaires were sorted by the 263 "neighborhoods" or census unit.

As new families moved into the district, the job of pupil registration took on new dimensions. No longer was it sufficient to enroll a pupil into a school; now the task was a continuous process of enrolling families into the school district.

A new, single-page form was developed for the census, replacing a sheaf of forms previously required. To provide the total pupil and family information required at various points in the school district, the one-page form was printed on a duplicator master, (See fig. 6) and the required number of identical copies (established by the number of children in the family) was produced cheaply and accurately.

The task of enrolling the large number of new families constantly moving into the District was assigned to a new enrollment office,

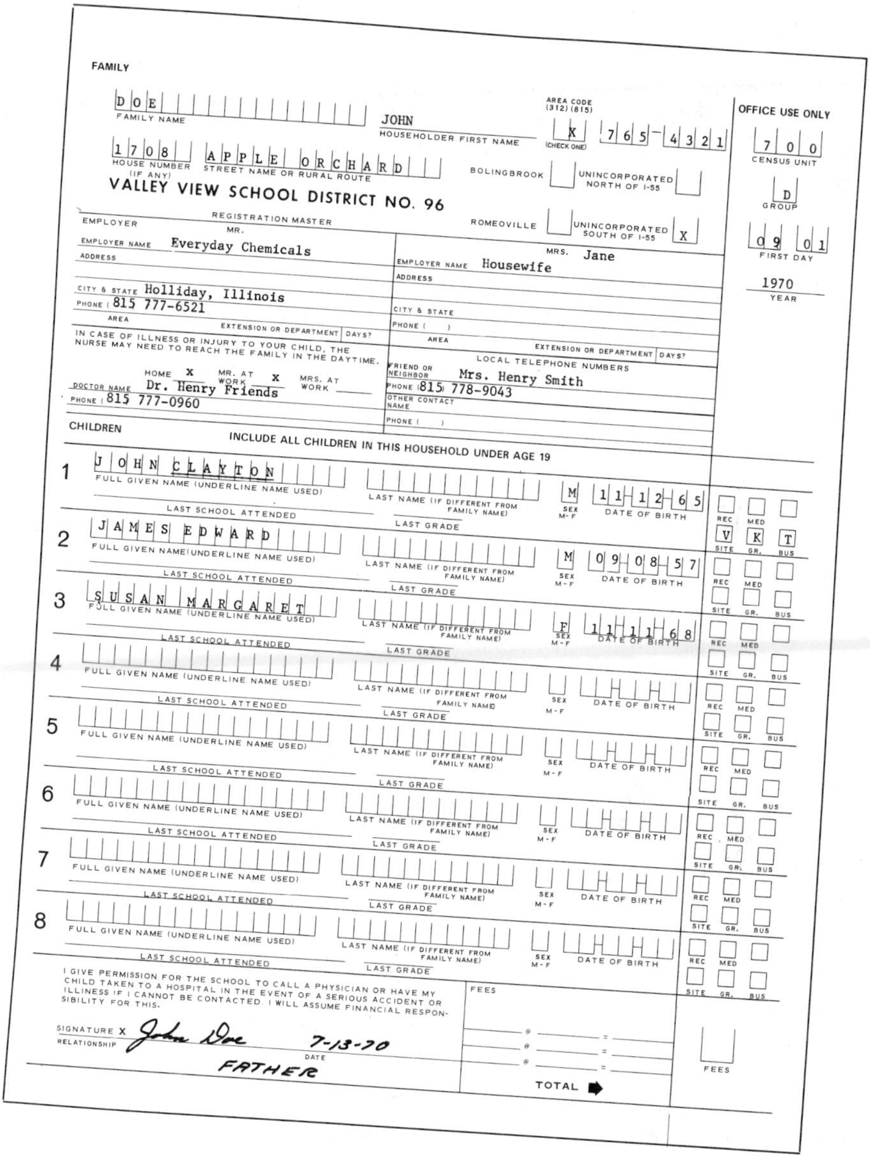

FIGURE 6. All information needed to enroll a family's children in school is obtained on this census form by the Valley View enrollment office. The compact one-page form is reproduced on a spirit duplicator master, permitting distribution of the data for various departments.

which served all of the schools of the District. The registrar explained the 45-15 calendar carefully, as well as collecting the pupil and family information needed and supplying the newcomers with other information about the schools and the Community.

For the initial "trial" scheduling, all that was needed was a count of the students and the preschoolers by age. However, it was essential to gather all of the pertinent information on the family, workplace, neighbors, doctors, etc. to prepare permanent records for the school District. The consultant recommended, but the District did not authorize, gathering housing data to aid in future enrollment projections.

WAR GAMES

Once the census data, taken in the spring of 1969, was combined with new enrollment information through the year, the District was ready to plan the master school schedule. This data was keypunched and tallied by computer for each of the neighborhood areas. As mentioned at the start of this chapter, the master schedule was simply a patient version of "Battleship" or "Tic-Tac-Toe." The process worked out in concentric circles, first taking into account the families nearest each school building.

Once the master schedule was built, the pupil schedules, class lists, notices to parents, assignment cards, and other information were prepared by Compumatics' IBM-360 computer.

When the scheduling by this "war game" process was completed, the superintendent was provided with a classroom planning worksheet (fig. 7) which showed the class sizes and grades offered for each classroom in the District, including the 60 which had been "created" by the scheduling process.

It was essential to schedule the children by concentric circles radiating from each building to insure:

1. That every child within walking distance (especially in kindergarten and primary grades) was sent to the nearest school.

2. That every building was utilized to capacity by those close to it, before children were bused between previous attendance zones.

3. That the school buses were utilized most efficiently. (This, incidentally, is a specific example of cost saving in the 45-15 system approach.)

From the cards it was also possible to produce a census summary by neighborhoods and age level, to determine accurately the building and transportation needs (fig. 8. Enrollment Summary Work Sheet).

The "test" pupil scheduling run was completed in November 1969, checked for accuracy, and used to address cards and letters mailed to each family in the district, notifying them of which "track" or group to which the children were assigned and which school and grade they would attend. Another pupil master list (fig. 9) was prepared in May 1970, for distributing final room assignments to parents and principals. This was supplemented by a similar "pupil transfer list," which informed each "sending" building of the names of students whose records would be transferred. "Pupil assignment lists" were prepared for each classroom, and served to guide enrollment, attendance reporting, and grade reporting.

ACCURATE MAPS NEEDED

An extremely important point in the schedule planning was the procurement of accurate maps of the two municipalities and all of the subdivisions in the unincorporated areas of the Valley View district. The lack of maps was, and still is, a standing joke. Actually Earl Thompson, who was employed to operate the Valley View bus pool, went out to all of the subdividers and local volunteer fire districts and accumulated a set of individual plats, which are mounted on one wall of the bus maintenance building adjoining West View Junior High School. The District still does not have an adequate master map to guide transportation and enrollment planning.

The authors have purposely avoided mentioning the special problems of scheduling West View Junior High School. The principal problem, here, of course, was that of taking into account individual student electives. Adequate programs for this scheduling assignment have been available, for a decade or more, at the college level, and will serve most secondary schools and junior highs, until they get into a rotating or staggered year-round enrollment plan. They then need the attention of a systems analyst to convert them to the particular local plan. The complication, of course, is that of integrating transportation and class assignments on the basis of family and neighborhood groups.

With the satisfactory completion of class assignments, little remained except the solution of transportation and maintenance problems. These will be covered in Chapter 12—"Dollars and Sense."

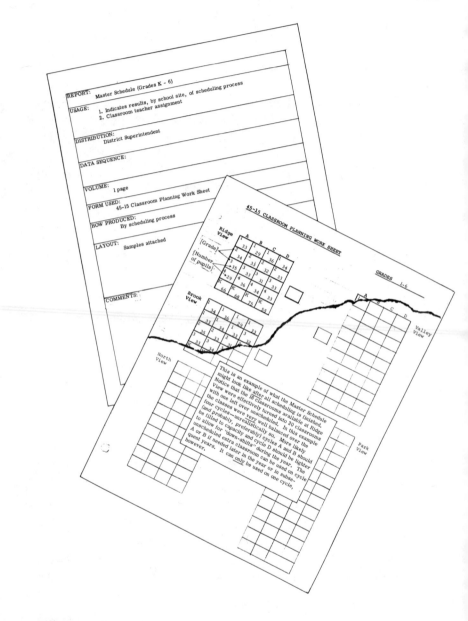

FIGURE 7. Essential to planning class assignments, transportation, and the use of facilities is a summary of student population for each age level, each building, and each attendance areas. These data are obtained from printouts from the basic census card, transferred to the classroom planning work sheet.

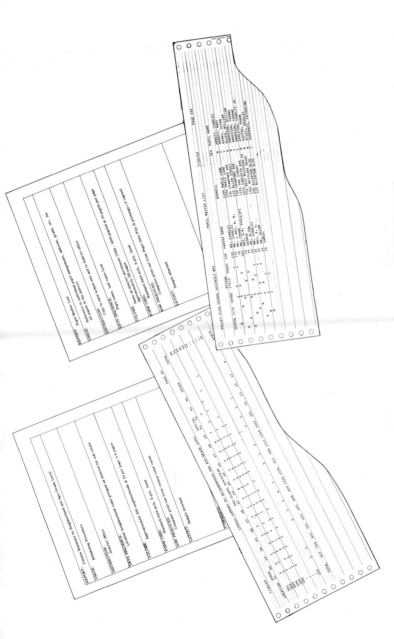

FIGURE 9. The pupil master list reveals final classroom assignments of each pupil. A transfer list also gives each "sending" school a directive for transfer of records.

FIGURE 8. The superintendent can determine building and transportation needs accurately from the enrollment summary work sheet.

11

Dollars and Sense

"How much money are you saving?"

This is the first question school board members ask, when they accompany their administrators on "fact finding" visits to the Valley View public schools.

The answer the Valley View administrators usually give is, "From two to five percent."

Then they explain that they cannot give a better answer until the audit of their 1970-71 fiscal school year is completed and certified to the board, usually late in the quarter ending September 30.

Of this amount, about two percent is in actual savings on bond and interest on new buildings, and about three percent is on the cumulative savings in instructional salaries, instructional materials, building maintenance, electric power (for heat, light and air conditioning), bus transportation, and the host of other costs that contribute to the total cost of education.

Businessmen are usually disappointed by the size of the estimated saving—particularly when the 45-15 Year-Round School Program creates a theoretical saving of one third in the size of the school plant since it increases the capacity of the existing school buildings by one third.

However, the cost-accounting-minded businessman must realize that he is dealing with many variables when he attempts to apply business management techniques to the school accounting systems and when he attempts to apply an exact dollar value to the savings experienced by any school system that adopts a Year-Round School program.

The authors have devoted many hours to producing answers for the Board of Education and will pass them along in this chapter. The analysis of these costs will be divided into two parts—capital costs, such as building construction, bond amortization and interest on building bonds—and operating costs, such as salaries, maintenance, transportation, light, heat, and air conditioning.

Before attacking the question of savings through fuller utilization of school buildings, it is well for the reader to understand the many variables that make an exact accrual accounting impossible.

ACCOUNTING PROCEDURE

Illinois follows an antiquated and complicated *cash* accounting system, which is specified by the State Legislature, and charges directly against each year's taxes the exact cash expenditures made during the fiscal year ended June 30. Taxes are collected (about 90 percent of them) in the following calendar year. Most Illinois school systems are forced to make substantial borrowings against taxes to meet their current bills, thus incurring substantial short term interest costs in both years being considered. District 96, in order to better inform its School Board and taxpayers, supplements the annual audit with a series of statements based on the more modern *accrual* method of accounting. Figures from the accrual set of books will be used in this analysis.

ATTENDANCE GROWS CONSTANTLY

Attendance is soaring constantly, 12 months out of the year. Under Illinois law, state aid to public schools is based on the controversial "average daily attendance" formula, computed on those children actually present during the best six months of the school year. District 96's official daily attendance increased from 5,166 at the start of the 1969-70 school year to 6,512 at the official start of the 1970-71 school year in September. (Students were enrolled in classes as early as June 30, under the 45-15 rotating school plan.) This increase included the addition of 768 kindergarten students (required of Illinois schools for the first time in the fall of 1970). By February 1 (midterm to most schools), actual attendance had increased to 6,950, a gain of 438 students over September. If this increase were extended to September, 1971, the official daily attendance for the opening of the 1971-72 official school year would be approximately 7,562, already well above the new theoretical capacity of the school district's buildings, even after adoption of the 45-15 year-round plan.

But this is not all. The 1968-69 recession in home building has apparently ended, interest rates on home mortgages are down, and new home sales are soaring again in all of the seven major subdivisions in the area. Sales are soaring particularly rapidly in a Bolingbrook subdivision that is offering condominiums with low monthly payments in the $16,000 to $19,000 price range, which is well below the price of the average home offered in the Chicago suburban area. The latest estimate, as of March 1971, is that attendance will increase nearly 3,000 during the 1971-72 school year. This will necessitate adding double sessions—as unpopular as they are—to the 45-15 program in June of 1971.

TEACHERS' SALARIES INCREASE 27 PERCENT

The average Valley View teacher earned $7,900 during the 1969-70 school year, last year when the entire teaching staff was on the traditional 180-day school year. The new contract negotiated with the Valley View Educational Association in the summer of 1970 established a $500 increase for the average teacher. (This increase, which amounted to a total of $106,500, includes the normal annual increment given teachers in most school systems on the basis of an additional year's experience.) However, this contractual increase does not take into account the additional days which teachers worked during the 1970-71 school year under the 45-15 plan. Chapter 9, on "Faculty," gives a good picture of the various contract years, which Valley View teachers are working. District 96 has awarded contracts—27 in all, ranging from 180 days to 274 days to fit individual teacher desires. Significant, however, is the average teacher salary for the 1970-71 year, which is $10,033.60, for a school year of 216 days. This average increase amounts to $2,133.60, or a total raise of 27 percent, comparing 1970-71 with 1969-70. Of this amount, at least $1,633.60 may be attributed directly to the extra income the average teacher is receiving under the 45-15 plan— an improvement of 19.5 percent in dollars. The truth lies somewhere between 19.5 and 27 percent, because it is possible that the faculty association settled for a smaller raise because of the significant increase in real dollar earnings. As a matter of practical comparison—

the contractual raise given Valley View teachers was $500 per year—
which compares with raises ranging from $500 to $800 for comparable suburban districts in the Chicago area. The reader must keep in
mind, however, that Valley View District 96 is a "poor district," and
would normally fall at the lower end of the scale.

In comparing teaching costs under the traditional nine months
school year and the 45-15 plan, the reader must keep in mind that
the district has continuously added teachers throughout the school
year to keep pace with soaring attendance. There is just no static,
"bench mark" point for which comparisons between years may be
made in a district of the same type as District 96. Comparisons may
be easier for a district which has stable enrollments. But that type of
district won't need to go to 45-15 anyway, except to phase out
antiquated buildings.

MAINTENANCE A STAND-OFF

In Illinois school accounting, custodial salaries, maintenance supplies, heat, light, and related contractual services are charged to the
educational fund. The total of operation and maintenance costs in
the 1969-70 school year was approximately $411,395.53. It will be
impossible to get a strict comparison between this last "conventional" year and the first 45-15 year, because two new buildings
came into use in the winter of 1970-71, with corresponding increases
in the custodial staff and power and light costs. However, the administration can say with confidence that there were no increases in
custodial staff and no substantial increases in maintenance overtime
because of 45-15. This should be important to those school administrators who constantly raise the spectre of "increased maintenance
costs" as a drawback to the Year-Round school. The District 96
answer is that hospitals operate 24 hours a day, seven days a week,
365 days a year. And they are usually spotless. Besides that, school
buildings are empty from 4 p.m. to 8 a.m. daily, plus Saturdays and
Sundays and the Christmas, Easter, and July 4th vacation periods.
All it takes to hold maintenance costs level is efficient management.
A detailed preventative maintenance schedule has helped District 96.

One more comment on maintenance and operations. The Valley
View schools are now all equipped with year-round, total-electric
heating and cooling. The power bills from Commonwealth Edison
indicate that summer cooling in the Chicago climate costs slightly

less than winter heating. This is just one more variable to complicate the formula. Each board member or administrator will have to determine his own capital costs and operating costs, depending on the provisions needed for air conditioning, and the type of heat for which the buildings are designed, electric, gas, oil, or coal.

BUS MAINTENANCE UP

Transportation is another place where the variations are hard to pin down. District 96, for reasons that had nothing to do with the institution of the 45-15 plan, switched from a private contractor to its own operation of school buses for the 1969-70 school year. The district purchased twenty buses (all 66-passenger models) at that time, and has handled the increase from 5,166 students in 1969 to 6,950 students, February 1, 1971, without the purchase of additional buses, or the employment of additional drivers or supervisors. The earnings of the bus drivers have increased, however, approximately 34 percent, since the drivers are now working 240 days a year, instead of 180 days a year. Earl Thompson, the District's transportation coordinator, points out that age, not mileage, is the principal element in figuring depreciation and resale on school buses, and so depreciation schedules may not change materially. However, maintenance costs may increase, with the additional mileage that the buses will put on each year under 45-15. In balance, the authors estimate that the transportation cost, which is a separate budget and tax levy item in Illinois, will probably increase proportionately to the increase in student population, especially in the second year of 45-15, when it may be necessary to add buses and drivers.

ADMINISTRATIVE COST DECLINE

Administration costs are again variables. District 96 added two principals in the 1970-71 school year to operate the two additional buildings. A third principal, or "educational leader," will be added for the new Oak View School, which will be completed in the middle of the 1971-72 school year. (More of this in Chapter 14, "Oak View".) However, these increases in educational leadership staff were made necessary by increased enrollment, not by the institution of the 45-15 plan. Turning the coin over, one might determine that the starting up of 45-15 eliminated the immediate need for two primary schools with the attendant cost of a complete staff of principal, secretaries, custodians, and other building-support personnel. It also deferred the planning of an additional junior high school or "middle school," a variation the district may need to consider.

However, there were additional costs attributable directly to the starting up of the 45-15 program at Valley View. J. Patrick Page was named assistant director of research, serving primarily to record the vast increase in information flowing into the superintendent's office, to work on scheduling, to answer the vast amount of correspondence that has been generated by the wide publicity given to the Valley View 45-15 Year-Round School program, and to assist in evaluation. Ronald Strahonoski was appointed assistant curriculum director at the start of the 1969-70 school year, largely to handle the additional load in negotiating individual teacher contracts on the basis of the number of days that teachers elected to work and to maintain constant communications with the faculty on all phases of the program. And so there have been increases required in District office administrative staff and clerical staff, traceable directly to 45-15. Any other school district implementing a similar plan would have to provide for some beefing up in the administrative office, at least for the short term.

Administrative help is a cost that each district will have to determine on the basis of actual work load. The authors must point out, of course, that the registration load has increased proportionately to the increase in enrollments. However, additional secretaries have not been employed in the individual school buildings. This is because the scheduling load has been handled entirely by computer, and because it is distributed every 15 days over the entire school year instead of being concentrated in the first few days of September. To further ease the load of the individual school building offices, the district opened a central "enrollment office" at the West View Junior High School, where a registrar interviews all parents of new students enrolling in the district; informs them of the 45-15 scheduling plan and the dates when and schools where their children shall report; and prepares the punch cards for registration, and the actual attendance folders for each child. This central office has held down the administrative costs in each building to manageable proportions.

Some of the communications load has been met by two small dissemination grants from the Illinois Office of the Superintendent of Public Instruction—$321.05 in December 1969, and $2,500 in

April 1970. In addition, the Superintendent of Public Instruction approved a Demonstration grant of $37,509.76 in July 1970 to care for the costs of demonstrating the 45-15 plan for the hundreds of school administrators and board members who have visited District 96, as well as paying guides to take them around to the various buildings in the district and provide them with "take home" information. These are not costs that accrue to most school districts undertaking a Year-Round school, but might be incurred to a lesser degree by the first Year-Round school in each region.

The Superintendent of Public Instruction also contributed $291 in December 1968 for a staff survey, and $750 towards consulting services for scheduling of students. The U.S. Office of Education, through its regional office in Chicago, appropriated $10,000 for a feasibility study (Project No. 9-E-112), which was completed in October 1970, and through its Washington headquarters approved a grant of $43,789.87 to start a continuing case study of the Valley-View district, devoted to student achievement, community attitudes and faculty performance, as well as finances. The current 45-15 evaluation project is funded by a $16,140 grant from OSPI. Chapter 13, "Way of Life," will offer more information on this case-study, "Planning a Year-Round Operation," (Project No. 0-0011). After taking all of these special costs and special studies into consideration, the Valley View administrators can only project an educated opinion that administration costs will not increase proportionately with enrollments under a Year-Round School program.

BUILDING SAVINGS IMPRESSIVE

Buildings, bonds, and interest—here, of course, is where the big savings may be obtained under the 45-15 Year-Round School plan. Theoretically and actually, the 45-15 plan increased the capacity of the Valley View school system from 4,800 pupils to 6,400 pupils—an increase of one third. Looking at the increase another way, the district was saved the cost of building two new school buildings, 60 classrooms at $28,000 each, including auxiliary spaces, or $1,680,000 each—a grand total of $3,360,000. The reader must remember, however, that this capital cost does not include the cost of borrowing $3,360,000 over approximately 20 years. This cost would bring the total cost of the two new school buildings to somewhere between $5 million and $6 million. Saved, also, were the cost of staffing and maintaining these buildings.

The exact amount of bonds and interest costs saved by the elimination (for now) of these two buildings depends on several additional factors. For one thing, District 96 sold its last bonds November 1, 1968, at interest costs ranging from 4.10 percent to 5 percent, depending on the length of maturity. During the following year school bonds for Class AA districts rose to slightly under seven percent, the new ceiling voted by the 76th Illinois General Assembly, and then dropped to slightly more than three percent in the spring of 1971. The true cost of the two new school buildings would have varied materially, because of the fluctuations in the money market. It is almost impossible to allocate a fair interest rate to an estimate of per pupil cost of the buildings, as the actual time of bond sale might have come at widely differing swings of the market.

There is still another important variable. At June 30, 1970, District 96 had available $5,867,070 in statutory bonding power. (In Illinois, an elementary district is permitted to issue bonds up to five percent of its assessed valuation, which was $117,341,413 on June 30, 1970.) There were $5,025,000 in district bonds outstanding, reducing the remaining bonding power to $842,000. The district simply could not have borrowed the money from traditional sources to build a single additional school building. The picture was slightly better at the end of the 1970-71 school year, on June 30, 1971. The estimated assessed valuation at this time, based on 1970 taxes, was $130,000,000. Approximately $310,000 in bonds were scheduled for retirement during the 1970-71 school year, reducing the bonds outstanding to $4,715,000. The bonding limit for 1971 comes out at approximately $6,500,000 (five percent of $130,000,000 assessed valuation). This leaves $1,785,000 in available bonding power. Enough to build one school with 30 classrooms, with a little to spare for other additions. Actually, all of the theoretical bonding limits should be reduced approximately 10 percent, to allow for shrinkage in tax collections. This shrinkage will be large in the 1971-72 year, because the new Illinois Constitution eliminates the personal property tax on individuals. Actually, District 96 sought, and received, relief from the State of Illinois through its emergency Illinois School Building Commission. This Commission approved granting Valley View a $1.7 million interest-free loan, repayable in 16 2/3 years, because it had exhausted its bonding power.

VOTERS ENDORSE BONDS

The District's voters also approved the sale of $845,000 in bonds, the limit permitted under law, on August 15, 1970. At that time, they also approved the "interest-free" loan of $1.7 million from the Illinois School Building Commission. The reader will learn more about this election in Chapter 13, "Way of Life."

The authors are sure that this long dissertation on local school finance will be interesting to school board members and administrators who are thoroughly informed on the complexities of public school finance. And it will be equally confusing to the layman. However, it does offer an adequate explanation of the many reasons why District 96's administrators can't offer an easy answer to the reader's obvious question, "How much money are you saving."

The authors can answer only that the savings amount from two to five percent for the current years and that they will loom larger as more bonds are amortized in future years. Each district will have to conduct its own feasibility study, either with its own accountants, a systems consultant familiar with the problem, or both. The title of this chapter is "Dollars and Sense." The authors might add that dollars and cents are secondary to the fundamental problem of educating children. The next chapter will attempt to deal with this paramount problem.

12

Kids

Kids are what school is all about.

The reader of this book might think that school administrators are concerned only with building and buses, maintenance, air conditioning, and tax referendums.

However, the Valley View schools would never have undertaken the 45-15 Year-Round School plan if the entire administration and staff were not convinced that there would be substantial educational gains for the children.

There has been little published research on the impact of the long summer vacation on learning. The early findings are inconclusive. Newark, Nashville, and Aliquippa all reported that there was no significant difference in performance between students attending the four quarters of the school year in those cities with rotating plans.

The consensus of most research is that students both regress and advance during the three-month summer vacation. Studies in New York and Florida tended to reveal that brighter, socially advantaged and economically advantaged students tend to continue to learn during the off-school months, but at a slower rate than they do when in school.

Probably the most significant research in the area of summer learning was conducted in the late sixties by Donald L. Beggs, assistant professor, department of guidance and educational psychology, Southern Illinois University, Carbondale. Noting that much previous research was inconclusive, because it was concerned with a single school, or a single class, Beggs conducted basic skills testing of fifth grade students in 32 Iowa schools after May 15 and before September 10 to measure any gains or regressions. The Iowa test of basic skills was used. Following is a table of average gains and losses between the May and September tests.

Table III
SUMMER LEARNING LAG*

Subtest	Percent Change
Reading graphs and tables	2.2
Map reading	2.0
Vocabulary	0.7
Reading comprehension	0.0
Knowledge and use of reference materials	0.0
Capitalization	-1.7
Usage	-1.8
Spelling	-2.0
Arithmetic concepts	-2.0
Arithmetic problem solving	-4.0
Punctuation	-5.0

*From: Research Applied to Practice, Illinois Journal of Education, January, 1969, pages 46-49, published by Superintendent of Public Instruction, State of Illinois, Springfield.

Beggs concluded that students lost the equivalent of five months of education in their basic language and arithmetic skills. He suggested that the gains reported in vocabulary, map reading, and reading graphs and tables might be a function of the family vacation.

Actually, Beggs was confirming statistically what every teacher knows intuitively. This is that basic skills must be reviewed for as long as one month each September before the teacher moves onto new curricular ground.

"The first and most obvious implication from the findings is that the teacher must be understanding of the general regression that occurs during the summer months," Beggs comments. "For this reason, the teacher should be willing to review the basic skills that are needed to succeed in the classroom for that year. . . . Once the basic skills have been relearned, the pupil should be better prepared to deal with higher level cognitive tasks. . . .

"A final implication to the educational community would be that it reconsider the present vacation schedule. The results of this study strongly suggest that the three-month vacation period is an interruption in the learning process. The knowledge explosion is of constant concern to the curriculum experts. One possible way of approaching the problem would be to spread the vacation periods throughout the calendar year such that no vacation period would be longer than four weeks."

STUDENT ACHIEVEMENT MEASURED

The Valley View administration has insisted, from the start, that adequate measurements be made of student performances and attitudes under the 45-15 program. Because any research in retention and growth of skills would be of benefit to the entire educational community, the U.S. Office of Education has funded a one-year study of learning in the Valley View schools to gather base line data.

William Rogge, associate professor of education at the University of Illinois, was retained to conduct surveys of community and teacher opinion, and primarily to collect "base line data" on the achievement of a representative sample of students in grades one through seven in the Valley View schools. Dr. Rogge is continuing the study under a grant from the Illinois Superintendent of Public Instruction.

A carefully selected sample of 736 students, grades one to six, was chosen to establish the base line for achievement. This sample was stratified for verbal intelligence, school, sex, attendance group, and grade level. All students were categorized for these "cells" and were then selected randomly. The researcher found no significant differences between students slated to join each of the school system's four attendance groups or "tracks." There was a significant variation in achievement in the first three grades of one school and in the performance of students new to the District. These will be considered in final evaluation of the tests.

The Metropolitan Achievement Tests (1959 Edition) by Harcourt, Brace & World, were administered to the primary and intermediate groups in June 1970. The Stanford Achievement Test, from the same publisher, was administered to the seventh grade pupils. All tests were administered under the Research director's supervision by two teachers with previous testing experience, thus eliminating any variations that might result through administration of the tests by the children's own classroom teachers.

The survey plan calls for continued testing over the next three years in both the Valley View schools and in another school system that follows a conventional calendar, selected to correspond as closely as possible to District 96 in socioeconomic composition.

Definitive results from these achievement tests and comparisons will not be available for approximately two years. When they are completed, they will contribute significant understanding to relative learning accomplishments of students under Year-Round schools, compared to those under traditional calendars.

Valley View's administrators were anxious to get some "straws in the wind," however. As the result, the administration commissioned J. Patrick Page, District research director, to secure some indication of evaluation of one factor, learning retention, during the first year.

Accordingly, on December 9, 1970, Page addressed a questionnaire to 88 classroom teachers in grades 1, 2, and 3. Since group "A" students were on vacation, teachers from this group were questioned on January 7, 1971, at the end of the Christmas holiday. The teachers were asked to check the statement that corresponded most closely with their subjective evaluation of student retention, with the following result.

Table IV
LEARNING RETENTION

Response	Number of Teachers	Percent of Teachers
a. A lot more retention	27	31
b. A little more retention	34	39
c. Unchanged	19	22
d. A little less	3	3
e. A lot less	0	0
f. No answer	5	6

(Five teachers did not answer, since they were new to the District.)

Page reports that there was no significant variation between teachers who were teaching "lock step" (45 days on and 15 off, with the students) and those who were teaching in "cooperatives," or rotating between classes.

Principals have reported no complaints from parents on student performance, and only a few who requested a change in their vacation schedule to fit in with family plans. Verne Shelley, principal at Park View School, reported after the first week of 45-15, "The students' attitude is just great; I would say at least 90 percent are happy with the program. Already they are remembering that they go nine weeks, and have three weeks off. I think they like the fact that they get four vacations a year."

Frank Kolinski, principal at West View Junior High, reported a common parent comment, "Thank God, the kids now have something to do during the summer."

William Dikeman, principal of the new Brook View School in Bolingbrook, reported, "The children seemed anxious to begin, and voted in favor of studying in air-conditioned buildings, and playing games indoors, rather than going out on the playground during the very hot days."

Linda McMillen, an eighth grader at West View, said, "It's really cool, and I mean that literally. I like keeping busy, and I used to get so bored before summer ended."

Brian Courtney, six, reported, "I missed recess while I was on vacation. I also miss going swimming. But Mom doesn't have a car, so we couldn't go anyway. It's easier to study than play outside in the hot weather. Mom likes 45-15, too, because she has more time to run errands."

The only serious objection to the whole program came from a group of mothers who held a meeting in August 1970 at the Park View School to complain that the 24 older rooms in the building were not air conditioned. Their children were moved into the air-conditioned part of the building, and the climate conditioning was completed in the older rooms during the 1970-71 winter period for use the following summer.

It seems only logical that children maintain their enthusiasm for school more easily when they can look forward to a vacation only nine weeks away, instead of nine months away.

Both children and teachers are keener and maintain their skills longer, under the 45-15, the authors hypothesize. Firm answers will be available as the three-year achievement research program is completed.

13

Way of Life

"The 45-15 Plan is a way of life in District 96; it's in no sense an experiment."

This is the way Ken Hermansen sums up the impact of the Year-Round School when he talks to visitors from other districts.

"The new school calendar has won virtually unanimous endorsement from students, parents and teachers in the District—both at the start of the program, and in retrospect, after completion of the first three 45-day quarters of operation," Hermansen summarizes.

The plan has also won remarkable interest and support from educators, editors, and laymen. The District had mailed out 3,930 information packets by March 31, 1971, with the aid of a grant from the Illinois Superintendent of Public Instruction. Each packet contains a 45-15 master calendar, an explanation of the plan and its advantages, comments by a board member, and an overall appraisal of the system by the educational director of the Illinois State Chamber of Commerce.

Visitors to the Valley View demonstration center in the West View Junior High School reached a total of 412 by March 31, 1970. Nearly half of these were administrators.

The demonstration center was established to insure a full presentation of the plan and all of its pros and cons for the many visitors who have come from across the country to form their own appraisals of the Valley View plan.

A breakdown of the registered visitors is shown in the following table:

Table V
TYPES OF VISITORS

Titles	Percent
Superintendents	10
Other administrators, including curriculum directors, assistant superintendents, and principals	38
Teachers	17
School board members	13
Laymen and press	12
Students, including college students	8
Federal and state education officials	2
	100

Each visitor first reviews a 15-minute film-slide and sound presentation that gives the setting, the rationale, and the District's experience with the plan in concise form. This is followed by a presentation and a question and answer period conducted by the director of the demonstration center, a teacher who has been assigned by the District to this federally-funded project. The visitors are then invited to lunch in one of the eight cafeterias in the district, primary, intermediate, or junior high. Here they have an opportunity to visit with teachers and building principals. After lunch, the visitors return for an additional question and answer period, conducted this time by the superintendent, one of the assistant superintendents, or the director of research. The questions asked by the visiting educators and laymen have given the authors a feeling of the pulse of the Year-Round school movement, and much of this book is devoted to answers to the questions they have posed.

The response from visitors has been most encouraging. They have found few "bugs" in the implementation of 45-15 at Valley View. The majority of the visitors, of course, have come from districts that have critical classroom shortage problems. Many of them have been unsuccessful in winning voter approval of needed bond issues for school building. It is significant that two school districts in the east were planning to implement the "45-15 Year-Round School Plan" in the Valley View format on June 30, 1971—less than nine months after they began their own feasibility studies.

As of June 1971, the authors have received definite confirmation that eight other school systems, ranging from New Jersey to Arizona, have already moved to implement the 45-15 plan, or a similar nine-week, three-week plan, on or about July 1, 1972. In addition, more than 100 school districts—elementary and secondary—have instituted serious feasibility studies of the Year-Round School Plan for possible adoption for the 1972-73 school year, or soon thereafter.

SIMPLE IDEA BREAKS ICE

Apparently one simple idea—that of breaking the long summer vacation up into four, three-week quarterly vacations—has broken the ice in favor of year-round education. This simple idea completely overcomes the overriding parental objection to the long-debated staggered four quarter plan—the long winter vacation and the long spring and fall vacations for three fourths of the students.

A professional assessment of 45-15 was made at a symposium conducted by the Educational Facilities Laboratories, Inc., an activity sponsored by the Ford Foundation, from September 24-26, 1970, at the O'Hare Inn, in Chicago. Following are some of the findings regarding 45-15, made by EFL's five consultants, who met with the architect for the innovative Oak View School on the final day of the symposium:

> —The 45-15 plan is a "terrific organizational plan" for increasing the utilization of school buildings, and has the greatest chance for continued success of any plan devised in the 65 years the nation has considered the school calendar problem.
> —The plan was born out of necessity, which increases its chance for continued success in District 96.
> —45-15 is basically only an organizational scheduling device. It has been used by District 96 to stimulate numerous innovative program developments. However, it should be understood by others who might use the plan, that it does not guarantee, nor necessarily require, innovative program developments any more than a hammer guarantees the building of a house. A hammer can also become an instrument of destruction.
> —The scheduling plan strongly encourages the adoption of team teaching, and, in fact, the plan's effectiveness is enhanced by the introduction of team teaching.
> —Many of the innovations encouraged by 45-15, such as team teaching and open space learning, do not depend upon 45-15 for success.
> —For continued success, the plan demands that community change and action take place, and that the schools adopt the community-school concept.

—School people must not delude themselves into believing that all learning must or should take place in the schools. Many community activities, including the home, must and do accept responsibility for many types of learning activities.

The EFL consultants also recommended a number of refinements in the plans for the Oak View School in Bolingbrook, which is the first school building in the country designed *specifically* for year-round education. These recommendations will be considered in Chapter 14, Oak View.

EFL's consultants also placed great stress on the 45-15 plan's role as a "catalytic agent" in developing better coordination of all of the community's quasi-educational and recreational activities. The device suggested by the consultants is formation of a "45-15" community council to plan year-round recreational activities for the students who are enjoying their three-week vacations each quarter. The Romeoville park district has prepared a 15-45 Recreational Program, but has been slow to implement year-round recreational facilities and activities to keep pace with the school system's 45-15 school program because of inadequate funding.

WOULD KEEP TEENS OCCUPIED

In discussing recreation, the authors might comment upon the special adaptability of 45-15 to high schools. Under this plan, as under the earlier "nine-three" staggered quarters plan, only one fourth of the students are on the street at any one time, a fact that has its implications for providing recreational activities that will help reduce vacation juvenile delinquency. Obviously buildings in use are less susceptible to vandalism than empty schoolhouses.

Valley View's experience with 45-15 has had a direct impact on secondary education in the Lockport area. The authors mentioned in Chapter 6, "Test-Tube," that District 96 falls within Lockport Township High School District 205, which operates three high schools in an area that straddles the Des Plaines River and the Illinois-Michigan Waterway. This district has been faced with many economic problems, compounded by the explosive growth of the communities on both sides of the Des Plaines Valley.

Parents in the Valley View District inquired of the District 205

Board why the Lockport West High School (in District 96) could not be operated on the 45-15 Year-Round plan, instead of on double-shifts. When they found the high school board unresponsive to their request, they began negotiations with the high school board, and with Boyd R. Bucher, Will County Superintendent of Schools, for division of District 205 into two independent high school districts. The negotiations, conducted by Harold Lindstrom, a former Valley View School Board member, were successful, and the boundaries of the district were adjusted on June 30, 1971, to give the Valley View communities elective control of Lockport West High School. As this brook is written, the new Board of Education for High School District 211 had not been elected, and a superintendent had not been chosen. However, there was a strong move in the community for closer articulation between the elementary and high schools, for possible implementation of the 45-15 plan at the secondary level, and for merging elementary and high schools in a "unit" district. Obviously, coordination of elementary and secondary school calendars in any single district, or area, chosen for implementation of the 45-15 plan would materially increase acceptance of this "way of life" by the Community.

When Valley View's administrators and the Board of Education undertook their year-round school program, no major curriculum changes were planned, or were felt to be needed. However, as the authors point out in Chapter 9, Teachers, the calendar has served as a catalytic agent in spurring an open-ended cycle of innovation on the part of individual teachers and small groups of teachers.

CURRICULUM STREAMLINED

Among the changes proposed by faculty members are:

1. The organization of curriculum into 45-day, self-contained units. According to Jamie McGee, president of the Valley View Education Association and chairman of the District 96 mathematics department, this would facilitate the acceleration of gifted students, or review of work incompleted by underachievers. Those who need to catch up with the schedule of work might have two choices. One would be to shift to the following group, thus losing 45 days in school progress, rather than an entire year, when they fail to pass.

2. The formation of "cooperative" groups of teachers, like the "team teaching" plan followed in many junior high schools. This has

taken place both among teachers who are working the long 240-day school year, and those who are following the lockstep 45-15 schedule with their students.

3. A sweeping reorganization of the whole curriculum to divide teaching materials into units of 45 days, or shorter duration, thus permitting formal grading and assessment of achievement at the end of each 45 day period, before the children go on vacation. This, in the opinion of the advocates, would give the entire school system greater flexibility, and greater ability to cater to the needs of individual students.

4. The organization of "repeater" or "tutoring classes" in which lagging students could "catch up" at the end of any 45-day period, by taking a few classes during their regular 15-day vacation.

The use of the 15-day vacation periods for special tutoring was recognized quickly by the Welch Learning Systems Company, of Skokie, Illinois, which contacted the Valley View administrators in the spring of 1970 and asked the District's blessing on opening a "15-45" tutoring school.

Welch opened its "Tutoring Center" in August, 1970, at the Good Shepherd Lutheran Church, a block north of the administrative offices in the Park View School, in Romeoville. As of March 31, 1971, the tutoring center had enrolled 82 Valley View elementary students and 23 Lockport High students and adults in a tutoring program that focuses primarily on the 15 days in which each group of elementary students goes on vacation. The Welch plan calls for keeping the students in the Tutoring Center for four or five hours a day during the vacation weeks, and for two to three hours a week during the regular 45 days of school. It is not a "baby sitting" service. The curriculum includes reading, English, speed reading, mathematics skills through three semesters of algebra, and post-high school mathematics and speed reading for adults.

The Welch Tutoring Center makes extensive use of programmed materials and learning machines and concentrates on individual and small group instruction. Tuition is on a flat two dollar hourly rate, with most programs focusing on a 35-hour total time budget. In keeping with the current educational trend to *accountability* through performance contracts, the Tutoring Center makes the following guarantee: "We guarantee to improve Reading, Math, or English skills by at least *one full grade level* upon completion of 35 hours of study. Additional instruction as may be necessary to achieve that level will be provided entirely free of charge by Welch Learning Systems—or a full refund of tutoring fees will be made." The authors do not necessarily imply that they endorse the Welch system, which is now conducted in more than 90 franchised and branch offices in the country. However, they agree with members of the Valley View faculty that 45-15 lends itself well to individualized instruction, to promotion of gifted students, and to less humiliating "catch up" programs for tardy learners.

As a catalyst, the 45-15 Year-Round school program, has served to focus attention on four trends already evident in the Valley View schools—individualized instruction, ability grouping, the ungraded school, and differentiated staffing.

The chemical impact of 45-15 on the faculty and on the educational thinking of the staff is best demonstrated in the program and plans for the new Oak View School in Bolingbrook, for which ground was broken in April of 1971.

The next chapter tells of the educational philosophies of the Valley View system, and their translation into bricks, mortar, and steel in the new Oak View School.

14

Oak View

No one in the Valley View schools foresaw the tremendous impact of the 45-15 Year-Round School Plan on the District's total educational program.

Administrators were confident that neither teachers nor children would suffer any adverse effects from calendar revision. In fact, they were confident that there would be small educational gains, due primarily to reduction of the long summer "learning lag."

As the authors have reported in earlier chapters, individual teachers and department chairmen turned to reorganizing the curriculum into four 90-day units, which would facilitate "short-term" deferment of promotion to students who needed to repeat work, as well as acceleration of gifted students without skipping an entire grade. The teachers also voluntarily formed teaching "cooperatives," groups of three or four, who were in effect adopting the team teaching plan. Still another result was a strengthening of the "ungraded school" concept, which had been followed by District 96 in the primary years.

Once the mechanics of the calendar revision plan and enrollment procedures were mastered, the administration turned to a searching appraisal of all of the educational ferment that was taking place in the District. Although the 45-15 plan had fitted easily into the District's existing school buildings, the administrators were determined that the next building in the District's program would reflect the fact that 45-15 had become a "way of life." Accordingly, they sought to incorporate the best of the faculty's educational innovations into the educational program and the architectural plans for the new Oak View School in Bolingbrook, to be occupied during the 1971-72 school year.

FIRST OF A KIND

Oak View was destined to become the first elementary school building designed specifically to house a year-round school and community program. This fact had sociological implications as well. Traditionally, schools have turned their students out for three months in the summer, thus placing a tremendous burden of recreational planning and supervision on the local park districts. To the Romeoville and Bolingbrook park system, 45-15 meant that there would be no summer rush from the entire school population; only one fourth of the children would be out of school at any one time (except for Christmas, Easter, and the end of June). The requirement, instead, would be for a continuous, year-round park recreational program, which logically would be located at the school grounds. The first requirement in planning the Oak View School, therefore, was that it become, in fact a "park-school," with both outdoor and indoor facilities for continuing day and evening community recreational programs.

The planning of the building itself was destined to be "different," because of curriculum philosophy, personnel utilization, and learning objectives.

Because of 45-15's built-in flexibility, the school system would be able to provide much more readily for individualization in teaching. The District 96 educational philosophy recognizes that each child passes through the stages of growth at his own rate. Each child's background of experience, his own potentials, and his rate of growth are unique to him. Consequently, there are wide differences of development and learning among children in every group. This recognition of individual growth created these implications for design and construction of the Oak View School:

1. Space design should facilitate various flexible arrangements of equipment and learning materials.

2. Space should be arranged to foster flexibility in the grouping of children.

3. Furniture and equipment should be suitable for children of different sizes and stages of development.

4. Facilities should vary in their challenge, use, and interest appeal.

The attention to individual growth and development led to physical building provisions that would foster:

1. Many kinds of meaningful experiences, related to each other, so as to strengthen and reinforce the pupils' learning.

2. Relatively free access to the entire building's resources, both indoors and outdoors.

3. Arrangement of equipment that would encourage a flow of activities, leading logically from one to another, in a sequence that would allow depth of learning and interest.

RECOGNIZES TOTAL GROWTH

The Oak View educational program recognizes also that the child's development is orderly, though uneven, and that it becomes more complex as the child grows. All facets of the school should then recognize the total growth pattern of the child, not just segments. The learning environment, therefore, should allow children to do many of the same things, as they progress, but on a more complex and co-ordinated level. Provision should be made, also, for children of different ages to engage in joint activities. Obviously, the facilities would have to provide for the children's obvious need for physical activity and for freedom to pursue their natural interests in the activities on view throughout the school.

The non-graded and cooperative teaching approaches have had direct impact on the planning of the building and its utilities:

1. The location, moveability, and absence of walls

2. The location of numerous mechanical (electrical and plumbing) outlets to facilitate movement of activities requiring them

3. The provision for gathering up to three normal sized (28 children) class groups into a single area for team presentations, audio visual, and other instruction.

The intended heavy use of audio-visual instruction also contributes to the design specifications:

1. By choice, window areas will be limited, to permit easier control of light.

2. Advanced acoustical control will be needed, to avoid a disturbing background level, and to avoid distraction of students in adjoining open areas.

It is obvious that air conditioning will be a prime requisite in the building plan.

The educational program also requires flexibility in staffing. Because the program calls for a high degree of individual instruction and the flexible grouping of children for various activities at various times, the Oak View School will rely to a great degree on teacher aides. In the following table is an outline of the tentative staffing of the school, which will house approximately 1,000 students.

Table VI

TENTATIVE STAFFING OF OAK VIEW SCHOOL

Activity	Teachers	Aides
Kindergarten	3	3
Primary	9	9
Intermediate	9	9
Physical education	2	
Art	2	
Vocal music	2	
Remedial reading	1	
Intermediate educable mentally handicapped	2	1
Speech correction	1	
Registered nurse	1	
Total	32	22

The Oak View educational program foresees that teachers will begin the first day of school with children organized in traditional groups of 28. (This class size is dictated by the regulations of the Illinois School Building Commission, which financed the building.) The administrators assume also that teachers in the primary and intermediate grades will organize into cooperative groups of three— probably one for each grade level. On the opening day of school, curriculum content will be essentially the same as children have followed in their previous school year assignments. There would be the usual emphasis on reading, language arts, arithmetic, science, social studies, prevocational courses, art, music, and physical education.

The planners hold, however, that the total layout of the school will allow the relocation and regrouping of educational tasks. One possibility would be division of the whole building into four learning functions—science, including the outdoors, humanities, social sciences, and problem solving area.

SEEK INDIVIDUAL INSTRUCTION

As the first school year proceeds, the administrators expect the Oak View School's staff to move toward more individualized instruction and toward greater use of the large, central learning center. The emphasis would shift from teacher-oriented activities to pupil-oriented activities. Students will be expected to keep track of their own academic progress, to do some of the program reporting to parents, and to help each other. *Responsibility* and *accountability* are to receive a very high priority in the pupil learning outcome.

The administrators expect that activities will be much more varied than in a traditional school. This requires that both space and equipment can be combined into a wide variety of patterns and layouts. "Nothing should be fixed, if it can be kept movable with reasonable cost and feasibility," Hermansen points out.

Flexible grouping of children will be fostered by greatly expanded evaluation of children through diagnostic tests and continuous reporting. Gradually, children will be taught how to keep records of their own progress, and how to make their own reports to their parents periodically. There will be constant evaluation of the total success of the program, through classroom profiles, and through leadership observation of the way teachers and students use their time.

NEW ADMINISTRATIVE LEADERSHIP

A significant facet of the program will be the restructuring of school administration. The principal will become an "educational leader," or a "master teacher," who will delegate all administrative routine to an assistant principal, while he concentrates on the quality of the educational program.

This educational concept of the school principal has captured the imagination of Dr. William Rogge, who in February, 1971, resigned his post as assistant professor of education at the University of Illinois to devote full time first to the 45-15 evaluation program and other Valley View research projects. On June 30, 1971, he became "educational leader" of the new Oak View School in Bolingbrook.

The architectural program that expresses the Oak View educational program is also unique. John W. Moore, executive director of the Illinois School Building Commission, took an active role in planning the Oak View School, visualizing the building as a place for innovations in construction, as well as innovations in education. Moore named an architectural-engineering team of individuals who had previously performed well in meeting low cost school building budgets. The design architect was Jack M. Goldman of Mount Vernon, Illinois. The participating engineers were Sangor Westphal, structural; William Peterson, mechanical; and Ronald Millies, electrical.

SCHOOL WITHOUT WALLS

The plan of the Oak View School is literally that of a "school without walls." (See fig. 10.) The only areas permanently separated from the rest of the school building are the kindergarten, the educable mentally handicapped classroom, the multi-purpose room, the conference room, counseling and administrative offices, kitchen, toilets, and storage areas. The learning center occupies a central area which may be expanded to take in the entire school. The open spaces are subdivided visually, but not by walls, to accommodate 150 beginning, 450 primary, and 420 intermediate students.

Because of the audio-visual requirements mentioned earlier, the building has very few windows. Special attention has been paid to the acoustical ceilings, the carpeting, the control of lighting, and the provisions for electrical and plumbing service to work areas. The entire building will be air conditioned, as are other Valley View schools. A "systems approach" of premanufactured building components will contribute to cost reduction and to flexibility.

The Valley View administrative team is confident that Oak View School and its educational program will be as innovative and flexible as the complementary 45-15 Year-Round School plan itself.

This chapter has contained the "lessons" that the Valley View administration has gained from the educational ferment triggered by adoption of the Year-Round School plan. The next chapter will treat with the "lessons" that administrators and others may gain from the total Valley View experience.

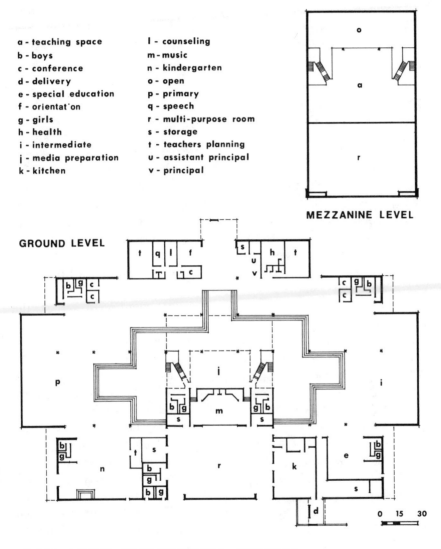

a - teaching space   l - counseling
b - boys   m - music
c - conference   n - kindergarten
d - delivery   o - open
e - special education p - primary
f - orientation   q - speech
g - girls   r - multi-purpose room
h - health   s - storage
i - intermediate   t - teachers planning
j - media preparation u - assistant principal
k - kitchen   v - principal

MEZZANINE LEVEL

GROUND LEVEL

OAK VIEW ELEMENTARY SCHOOL

FIGURE 10. Oak View Elementary School is designed for flexibility in its educational program.

15

Lessons

Valley View's administrators do not consider 45-15 a cure-all for school ills. But scores of school administrators and school board members who have visited District 96 during the past year agree that the 45-15 Year-Round School plan is the most workable, most viable form of calendar revision that has been proposed.

As this book is written, Valley View District 96 is the only school system that is following a year-round school calendar throughout its buildings. (The Becky David School in the Francis Howell school district, St. Charles, Missouri, is operating a 45-15 plan in a single primary and intermediate school.)

The administrators of Valley View have learned lessons that will prove helpful to other school administrators and board members, who may be seeking to solve their school housing problems by some form of a year-round school calendar. However, the authors realize each school district has its own problems and its own circumstances that may dictate solutions different from those worked out at Valley View. However, for what they are worth, the authors pass along their observations on 45-15, as followed at Valley View, and other year-round proposals that have been advanced in other areas.

First, the authors should make clear that the 45-15 Year-Round School plan is simply a revision of the school calendar. It does not change the total number of days that students attend school. Each student attends classes for a total of 180 school days, just as he would under a traditional school calendar.

However, the long summer vacation of three months is split up into four short vacations of three weeks duration each, which are scheduled in the fall, the winter, the spring and the summer. In addition students and teachers enjoy the traditional Christmas and Easter holidays, and an additional week or 10 days off at the end of June.

The 45-15 school calendar does increase utilization of school buildings by one third. Three fourths of the students are in school at any one time, while the fourth group of students is on the three week (15 day) vacation. Thus the 45-15 plan gains greater use of school buildings solely through efficient year-round scheduling, instead of letting them remain idle for three months during the summer.

The 45-15 Year-Round School plan must be distinguished clearly from the staggered four-quarter plans, or from extended year plans. The staggered four-quarter plans stay with the traditional three-month vacation period, except that one fourth of the students are let out for a full three-month vacation in each season—the fall, the winter, the spring, or the summer. The authors are firmly convinced that parents will kill any staggered quarter plan, just as they did in Aliquippa and Ambridge, Pennsylvania, in the late thirties. After all, "Who wants to see kids out on the streets for three months in midwinter?"

The extended year plans are generally an extension of the familiar summer school programs—except that they usually last for fifteen weeks instead of eight. Most extended year programs are voluntary—at the most, they have attracted from one fourth to one third of the total school enrollment. They do not achieve an increase in the total number of classrooms available to house the enrollment—the principal gain of 45-15.

The 45-15 Year-Round School plan is not an acceleration of "speedup" plan. It does not rush kids through school, to graduate a year or two before they are intellectually, physically, and socially ready for completing either elementary or high school. On the other hand, the 45-15 calendar does allow for a modest amount of student promotion or review in exceptional cases with relatively little disruption of their progress through school.

POPULAR WITH TEACHERS

Teachers generally like 45-15. They have the option of working for only 180 days a year, either rotating class days and vacation days as their pupils do. Or they may work as many as 240 days or 274 days (the schedule worked by Eileen Ward, the senior teacher in the Valley View district). Two out of three teachers in the Valley View schools have elected to work more than 180 days a year, electing some 27 different contract terms. The average Valley View teacher earned 27 percent more during the 1970-71 school year than he would have earned under a conventional school calendar. Male teachers, especially, like the longer contract year, which enables them to work at their dignified profession all year, instead of seeking part-time jobs in less rewarding summer work, as the traditional school calendar often requires.

The 45-15 plan does not necessitate a change in curriculum. Valley View schools were sending grades home with children four times a year, which coincide with the four 45-day quarters in school. Although no curriculum changes were planned at Valley View, both teachers and department chairmen were inspired by the major calendar revision there to undertake a major assessment of the curriculum. This in turn led to major changes in school organization and a refinement of educational philosophy. These were unexpected positive by-products of 45-15—not goals of the calendar revision program.

From their experiences at Valley View, and their observations of the other year-round school proposals, the authors offer the following lessons and observations:

HOW TO KILL A YEAR-ROUND SCHOOL PLAN

1. Send out a community questionnaire, asking the people, "Do you want a year-round school?" They'll tell you, "No!"

2. Form a large study committee of lay people, and study the problem to death. (This was the experience of the Jefferson County schools, in the suburbs of Louisville, Kentucky.)

3. Attempt calendar revision with a board that is strongly divided —some for the year-round school; some against it; and some with no commitment. Batter the problem to death in open school board meetings.

4. Go to Atlanta, Gerogia, and come back with the finding, "Year-round school costs $2 million a year to operate, and our district can't afford it!" (Atlanta schools and Fulton County schools, in Georgia, offer an *extended* school year, with fifteen extra weeks of classes, which are attended by about one third of the students. The

Atlanta plan has little chance of adoption in any areas where the public is not committed to spending "more money" on schools, not less.)

HOW TO SUCCEED

There are three main ways to succeed. They all have to work together:

1. Have a board of education and an administration committed to attacking a year-round school program, and approach the problem and proceed in a businesslike manner.

2. Continue an organized community relations program, involving the total community, not only for the year-round school, but for all ongoing school problems.

3. Develop a plan that will suit the purposes and problems of your particular district. And don't expect any present year-round program (including 45-15) to be "plugged in" to your type of school operation 100 percent.

Here are some of the by-products you may and may not expect from a calendar revision program, such as 45-15:

1. Expect to reduce teacher turnover, Your better paid teachers, in particular, will stick with you.

2. Expect learning retention to improve. That's the opinion of 70 percent of the teachers in the first three grades of the Valley View schools, after five months of experience with the 45-15 plan.

3. Expect more flexibility in individualized instruction. Teachers will be willing to hold up slow learners for 45 days, when they might be unwilling to set children back a full year. Likewise, teachers will be willing to accelerate rapid learners by 45 to 90 days, when they might be unwilling to move children ahead by a full year. The time gained can always be devoted to further enrichment of the "gifted" students.

4. Don't expect to save money on teachers' salaries. Teachers will expect that they get paid at the same daily rate for winter and summer.

5. Don't expect spectacular savings in year-round operating costs. Some costs will go up; some down. The big saving, of course, is the cost of building and financing the new school buildings you will not need. Also expect to make savings in the salaries of the extra administrators, secretaries, nurses, and custodians to staff the buildings you do not build.

6. Expect that teachers may at first mistrust your motives in considering calendar revision. Level with them. Let them know that they will be paid at their full daily rate during the summer months, and that their retirement-pension benefits will be increased proportionately to their extra earnings.

7. Iron out any differences you may have with your teachers' organizations *before* you undertake a calendar revision program. Don't let any old grievances muddy the waters.

8. Expect better utilization of libraries, books and equipment; but expect greater wear on books. Most of them will be outdated before they are worn out, anyhow.

9. Expect total transportation costs, including maintenance costs, to increase. But busing costs per pupil may decline. Bus drivers will generally be paid one third more money each year. Depreciation of vehicles is a factor of age, not mileage.

10. Expect no serious difficulties with maintaining school buildings under a year-round program. After all, hospitals stay open 24 hours a day, seven days a week, 52 weeks out of the year. And they're generally cleaner than schools. In addition to afternoons and evenings for scheduled maintenance work, there are still three significant periods of time when no children or teachers will be present (Christmas, Easter, and the end of June) in which major maintenance work can be performed.

11. Make your year-round school plan compulsory; but make minor concessions in scheduling to fit the vacation plans of individual families. Only 24 families out of 6,000 requested a change in group calendar assignments at Valley View.

12. Be sure that all of the children in one family belong to the same group and that they attend school on the same days. Do the same for all of the children in a single neighborhood. It keeps schoolmates together, and it makes it easier for parents to trade off baby sitting chores.

13. Finally, let the school calendar revision plan stand on its own feet. Even though you may foresee some curriculum changes, don't tie the school calendar change up to teacher negotiations, a new educational program, tax referendums, or school board elections.

These are the lessons that have helped make Valley View's 45-15 Year-Round School plan a success. These lessons may prove helpful to other elementary, secondary and unit (unified) districts contemplating calendar revision.

Overview

There is no doubt that 1970-71 is the school year in which the "great debate" over year-round education ended—the year in which action began, on a nationwide scale.

As the school year ended, two school systems in the east had adopted the 45-15 Year-Round School plan, with less than one year's preparation, and were planning to introduce their first groups to the new calendar on July 6. These were:

1. The Champlain Valley High School District, with approximately 800 students, fed by five elementary school districts, in the countryside surrounding Burlington, Vermont.

2. The Prince William County schools, in Virginia, which were planning to implement the 45-15 plan for approximately 2,500 rural school children in the area surrounding Gale City, an area impacted by the families of officers and enlisted men stationed at the nearby United States Marine Corps base at Quantico.

Administrators of eight school districts, ranging from New Jersey to Illinois, to Arizona, and to California, had reported to Valley View that their school boards have authorized implementing year-round programs to begin with the 1971-72 year. Each of these systems was allowing the full year the authors feel to be necessary to adequately prepare for a major calendar shakeup.

Well over 400 school administrators, board members, teachers and educational writers have visited the 45-15 Demonstration Center in the West View High School in Valley View District 96. A poll of these visitors indicated that more than 100 school districts across the country are seriously studying implementation of a 45-15 plan, or a similar year-round program, during the 1972-73 school year.

STATE DEPARTMENTS ACT

State departments of education in New Jersey, Vermont and Virginia are making comprehensive studies for the guidance of their local public school districts, as well as preparing legislation amending their school codes to facilitate the institution of year-round programs.

Further indication of the growing interest in calendar revision came from attendance at the Third National Seminar on Year-Round Education, held March 24-26, 1971, in Cocoa Beach, Florida. Interested participants came from thirty states and three countries. There were 360 school people registering from addresses outside of Brevard County, Florida, home of the conference. The three-day program furnished an overview of both compulsory and voluntary "enrichment" progress. Valley View presented a panel discussion five times, which included the administrators, a teacher, a student, and a member of the Board of Education, as well as eager questioners from the audience.

CHICAGO MOVES AHEAD

By far the most comprehensive development, however, concerns the giant public school system of the City of Chicago.

On March 24, 1971, the Chicago Board of Education approved the second phase of a year-old study that would carry to eight high schools and 46 elementary schools the discussion of year-round programs.

General Superintendent of Schools James Redmond recommended involving district superintendents, local school staffs and teachers, and organized community councils in the evaluation of four district school calendar revision programs:

1. The long-debated and dormant staggered four-quarter plan, in which students would attend school nine months and stay home three.

2. The 60-20 day, or 12-week, 4-week, plan long advocated by Mrs. Mary Liebman of McHenry, Illinois.

3. The 45-15 Year-Round School plan, as followed at Valley View during the 1970-71 school year.

4. The 8 a.m. to 10 p.m. Flexible High School plan, which would permit some high school students to work full time during the day, and attend high school in the evening.

A comprehensive study, developed by Dr. Joseph Hannon, assistant superintendent of facilities planning, and the department of educational program planning, recommended that local councils of citizens, administrators and teachers be given "freedom of choice" in electing the plans to serve their communities.

Annual costs of the Chicago program—to be implemented in "July or September" of 1972—were estimated as follows:

Additional teachers' salaries	$8.1 million
Air conditioning of 20 of the 54 schools under consideration each year	2.1 million
Extra maintenance costs	14.3 million
Programming ($70,000)	

The total annual cost for the 1972-73 year was estimated at $27.2 million. There will also be some air conditioning, maintenance, and programming costs to be incurred during the 1971-72 school year. However, it is anticipated that these costs will be more than offset by future savings in construction costs, fringe benefits saved by employing fewer teachers due to existing teachers, in many instances, teaching a longer school year, savings on additional administrative and clerical staff, and the like.

Dr. Redmond and his assistants plunged immediately into conducting the local informational campaigns in a dozen or more sections of the city.

The actual schools scheduled for the intensive study were selected on the following criteria:

Severe reading needs.
Integration needs.
Bilingual needs.
Multi-ethnic needs.
Severe crowding.
Rapidly increasing enrollments.
The convertibility of the buildings selected for implementation.

Dr. Redmond's proposals were supported strongly by all four of Chicago's metropolitan daily newspapers, which had previously reported on the 45-15 Year-Round School program at Valley View and had endorsed it editorially. Both news and editorial support was given to Dr. Redmond's program by all three network-owned television outlets in the city. As this book went to press, there was every indication that both the Chicago Board of Education and the Chicago Federation of Teachers would lend their continuing support to the intensive program of educational study and community involvement that is regarded as an essential foundation to Chicago's year-round program.

Initial enthusiasm for Chicago's year-round school program was high, so high, in fact, that plans were drafted to start 45-15 programs in nine elementary schools in the summer of 1971. Plans for rushing these nine schools into a year-round program were deferred until 1972, however, when it became apparent that the majority of the parents concerned had not fully endorsed the program.

NIXON, FINCH, HUMPHREY

Endorsement of the principle of Year-Round Education came from high places.

President Richard Nixon told the 91st Congress of the United States, in his message on education of March 19, 1970, "There is a need to stimulate more efficient and less expensive (educational) administration by better management of financial resources that can reduce capital investment needs, and the use of school facilities year-round."[1]

Robert H. Finch, now Counselor to the President, and then Secretary of Health, Education and Welfare, in 1969 told the American Society of Newspaper editors that the nation needs to develop a new concept of community education centers, sharing facilities with community colleges.[2]

"The same impulse moves us in the direction of experimental schools—'round the clock, 12-month community learning centers,' starting with the elementary grades and running across the whole educational spectrum," Finch said. "We conceive of these schools as the focal point for infusing the concerns, the special needs, the skills of the entire community into the educational system—schools in which community input is every bit as important as the product.

"We are thinking of such schools in direct, intimate association with community colleges . . . indeed, they might even share the same campus at times, and their elementary and secondary classrooms might be developmental laboratories for those community college students engaged in teacher training, or retraining."

Senator Hubert H. Humphrey of Minnesota, who opposed Richard Nixon in the 1968 presidential election on the Democratic ticket, in 1971 added his voice for year-round education.[3]

"We must all work to make greater utilization of the educational facilities which sit idle for many months of the year . . . Our educational facilities must be recognized as a valuable resource. We must take full advantage of their use to reap a full return on our investment," Senator Humphrey wrote the authors.

The authors of this book believe that these highly placed commentators were primarily reflecting the increasing general national concern for greater *efficiency* and *accountability* in the administration of the nation's public and private schools.

Educational Digest reported that public approval of school tax and bond referendums dropped to less than 50 percent of the issues presented during the 1969-70 school year. Dr. George Gallup, in his annual poll of public opinion of the schools, reported that support was at its lowest point in recent years.

Most life-long workers on the educational scene believe strongly that this apparent disaffection with the schools is primarily an expression of displeasure over mounting federal, state and local taxes, and the menace of inflation. They point out that only at the school referendum does the voter ever get an opportunity to express his opposition to taxation; and the schools suffer.

Whatever the cause, it is apparent that the school system must roll with the punches. The successful experience at Valley View demonstrates that significant improvements in both education and economy may be made by a new look at the school calendar, and at the organization of the curriculum.

The time for bold, forward-looking change has truly come.

Bibliography

Chapter 1
1. Wirt, William A. *A School Year of 12 months.* Education, 1907.
2. *Newark, New Jersey Year-Round Schools.* Newark, N.J. Public Schools, 1932.
3. *The All-Year School of Nashville, Tennessee.* Field Study Number Three, George Peabody College for Teachers, Nashville, 1930.
4. Vanderslice, H. R. *The All-Year School in Aliquippa, Pennsylvania.* Elementary School Journal. March, 1930.
5. Vanderslice, H. R. *Five Year's Experience With the All-Year-School.* Elementary School Journal, 34:256-268, December, 1933.
6. Irons, H. S. *Utilizing School Buildings and Instructional Services 12 Months Annually.* American School Board Journal, March, 1934.
7. Beveridge, J. H. *Omaha High School on the All-Year Plan.* School Life. 11:22, October, 1925.

Chapter 3
1. *Los Angeles Rejects Plan for Keeping Schools Open Year-Round; Calls It Costly.* Nation's Schools. 55:120,112, February, 1955.

Chapter 4
1. Rice, Mary Tomancik. *Administrators Dispute Arguments for All-Year Schools.* Nation's Schools. 47:69-71, June, 1951.
2. *Opinion Poll: Superintendents Reject All-Year School Plan;*

Teachers and Buildings Need Three Months to Recoup and Repair. Nation's Schools. 35:6, May, 1955.
3. Engh, Jeri. *Why Not Year-Round Schools.* Saturday Review. 49:82-84, September 17, 1966.
4. Friggen, Paul. *Why Not Year-Round Schools.* Reader's Digest, Vol. 74, p. 87, May, 1959.
5. Ingh, Jeri. *Case for Year-Round Schools.* Reader's Digest. 89:141-144, December, 1966.
6. Fitzpatrick, Dave. *Why Nova School Switched to Three 70-Day Trimesters.* Nation's Schools. 77:4, April, 1966.
7. Wehmhoefer, Roy. *The Twelve-Month School Year—A Study of the Advantages and Disadvantages of the Four Quarter System.* Cook County Superintendent of Schools, Chicago, 1968.

Chapter 5
1. Thomas, George I. *Economy and Increased Educational Opportunities Through Extended School Year Programs.* The University of the State of New York, The State Education Department, Office of Research and Evaluation, Albany, New York, 1965.
2. Thomas, George I. *Extended School Year Designs: An Introduction to Plans for Rescheduling the School Year.* The University of the State of New York, The State Education Department, Office of Research and Evaluation, Albany, New York, 1966.
3. Thomas, George I. *The Impact of a Rescheduled School Year:* A special report prepared for the Governor and the Legislature of the State of New York. The University of the State of New York, The State Education Department, Albany, New York, 1970.
4. *Extended Summer Segment, Make-Up Segment.* Hornell Senior High School, Hornell, New York, 1966.
5. Beggs, Donald L. *The Summer Vacation—An Interruption in Learning.* Illinois Journal of Education, Springfield, January, 1969.
6. Thomas, George I. *What is the Continuous Learning Year Cycling Plan?* The University of the State of New York, The State Education Department, Office of Research and Evaluation, Albany, New York, 1970.
7. Johnson, Oz. Speech at First National Seminar on Year-Round Schools, Fayetteville, Arkansas Public Schools, 1968.
8. Gillis, Reid. *The Twelve-Month School Year; Plans and Strategy.* Education Summary, September 1, 1968.

9. Education, U.S.A., March 8, 1971. National School Public Relations Association, Washington, D.C.
10. Glinke, George B. *The Extended School Year: A Look at Different School Calendars.* Utica Schools, Utica, Michigan, April, 1970.
11. McLain, John D. *The Flexible All-Year School.* Research-Learning Center, Clarion State College, Clarion, Pennsylvania, 1969.
12. Beckwith, Robert A. *The Challenge of Romeoville.* Current Report, Illinois State Chamber of Commerce, Chicago, January, 1970.
13. Hamilton, Charles. *A Financial Evaluation of Becky-David Year-Round School.* The Danforth Foundation, St. Louis, Missouri, 1970

Chapter 16
1. President Richard M. Nixon, Message to Congress, March 19, 1970, The White House, Washington, D.C.
2. Robert H. Finch, remarks presented at the American Society of Newspaper Editors Luncheon, April 18, 1969, Washington, D.C.
3. Senator Hubert H. Humphrey, letter to Hal Burnett, February 18, 1971, Washington, D.C.